FOOLPROOF

PICNIC

FOOLPROOF PICNIC

• PICNIC •

60 DELIGHTFUL DISHES TO ENJOY OUTDOORS
MARINA FILIPPELLI

PHOTOGRAPHY BY
LAURA EDWARDS

Hardie Grant

QUADRILLE

Managing Director
Sarah Lavelle

**Commissioning
Editor**
Stacey Cleworth

**Art Direction
and Design**
Emily Lapworth

Photographer
Laura Edwards

Food Stylist
Marina Filippelli

Prop Stylist
Louie Waller

Head of Production
Stephen Lang

**Senior Production
Controller**
Nikolaus Ginelli

First published in 2022 by Quadrille,
an imprint of Hardie Grant Publishing

Quadrille
52–54 Southwark Street
London SE1 1UN
quadrille.com

Cataloguing in Publication Data: a catalogue
record for this book is available from the
British Library.

Reprinted in 2022
10 9 8 7 6 5 4 3 2

9781787137936

Printed in China

CONTENTS

INTRODUCTION

The secret to a foolproof picnic? Surround yourself with good people, good food and let the drinks flow generously. Yes, it's that easy. Oh, and embrace the mess...

As a kid, I loved picnics. If I'm honest, I have little memory of the food itself; it was the general carefree, rule-breaking nature of them that spoke to me. Want to run around between mouthfuls? Fine. Want to eat with your hands? Great, we forgot the cutlery, anyway. Spilt your drink? Well, it's a picnic, it was bound to happen to someone.

As a bit of a control freak, I try to remind myself of this when putting together a picnic. Once you've committed to eating outdoors, you have to be prepared that however well organized, there is every chance that nothing will go to plan, so you might as well go with the flow and have fun with it.

The food: keep it simple

The trick, as with most things, is to keep it simple. I equate picnics with lazy days: sitting in a park, meadow, on a beach or even in the garden, soaking in the sounds of nature, and of people relaxing and playing nearby. So why not get into the mood with some lazy cooking too? Choose food that you can prepare with pleasure, without stress, and avoid trying to do too much. You really don't need to bust a gut in the kitchen for hours – unless that's what you enjoy, in which case go for it!

I generally focus on one more-involved dish that might take a bit of effort, such as the Walnut, Parsley and Sundried Tomato Babka on page 92 or a tart of some sort, then pair it with, say, a salad that calls for minimal input, such as the Courgette, Chickpea and Feta Salad (see page 37), or Parma Ham and Buffalo Mozzarella with Spring Vegetables (see page 42). And if I'm tired, busy, or just haven't had the time, then I might make only one dish, then pick up some bread, cheese and other deli bits on the way. All you need is delicious food that can be transported easily and that will keep well outdoors.

It's also worth reminding yourself that a picnic is not like entertaining; you don't have to do it all. The bigger the picnic, the less work you need to take on yourself. If everyone comes bearing a dish, drink or punnet of fruit, it will figuratively and literally lighten your load. After all, you can only take what you can comfortably pack and carry.

Pick a great spot

Whether you're after a beautiful view, a romantic spot by a stream or a pretty-enough corner as close as possible to the car park, take your time to choose it. I always look for somewhere with a little shade from a tree if possible, on ground that's dry and flat enough and – most importantly – has an engaging view, provided either by nature or interesting people-watching opportunities. Once you've found what you're after, check for any undesirables. From painful experience, I can most definitely confirm that it's better to notice that ant nest before setting up camp, rather than after you've disturbed it.

What to pack

As you can see flicking through the pages in this book, I'm not a great believer in buying special picnic kit. Invest in a fancy picnic blanket or basket with plates and cutlery if you like, but they are not necessary and can be heavy and cumbersome to carry.

Picnic blanket

I find woollen blankets can be itchy, so I will often opt for a large cotton tablecloth or towel. They are light and not too bulky, making them easy to carry – plus they can conveniently go in the washing machine once you get home. The bigger the better, so nobody ends up sitting over the edge and, if you're planning a large get-together, remind everyone to pack one for themselves and make a patchwork as your party grows.

Baskets and cool-bags

Most of the recipes in this book will sit well at room temperature unless it's an excessively warm day, so they can travel safely in any basket or bag. You'll need a cool-bag for drinks, though. My favourites are the large soft cool-bags that aren't too heavy. I put a large bag of store-bought ice inside as a base, then add the cold drinks and sit any fruit and bags of salad leaves or herbs on top.

Find a shady corner when you get to the picnic and the ice should keep everything cool for hours, even after you've stolen some cubes to add to drinks. Before you head home, tip out any leftover ice (or water if it's all melted).

Packing and serving the food

There are no right or wrongs here. If you're driving somewhere with picnic tables, this is your chance to go to town; otherwise, stick to the basics and pack light. Some people like to pack everything in airtight containers that guarantee no spillage, but I also like to use baking sheets, baking trays (sheet pans), or roasting tins (pans) to carry things safely, especially delicate or creamy dishes.

Jam jars are great for serving dips and dressings, and if there are any spare hands for carrying, I sometimes take one of the dishes on a pretty serving platter or board that I can just sit on the picnic blanket, ready for digging in.

Ceramics are only feasible if your picnic spot is a couple of minutes away or if you're driving. Otherwise, enamel bowls, or any other light metal dishes, are possibly the most practical, with the added benefit that there's no chance of breakage. And, of course, look out for melamine and bamboo dishes, which are light, hardy and a good sustainable option.

You'll also need

Plates, glasses and cutlery
If it's a big gathering, or one with lots of kids, paper plates, glasses and napkins are your friend; otherwise I'm not a fan of disposables. Again, go for light, sustainable unbreakables if you can, then add anything you don't mind chipping...

Chopping board
To use as a clean surface to serve food on, and for slicing or chopping.

A large sharp knife
There's always something to slice or chop.

Corkscrew and bottle opener
Obviously.

Roll of kitchen paper
For those inevitable spillages and for when the napkins run out.

Cushions
Somewhat of a luxury, these will keep you comfortable, especially if it's promising to be a long loungey day. Like those travel pillows people wrap around their necks on long-haul flights, a cushion might seem excessive, but you'll never regret having one with you.

Rubbish (garbage) bags
Not just for your rubbish, but also use one to collect all the dirty crockery so you don't end up with a mucky picnic basket.

Games
A Frisbee, football (soccer ball) or beach bats. Because is it even a picnic if at some point you don't split into the 'sporty group' and the 'time for a nap group'?

Key

Vegetarian (V), vegan (VE) and pescatarian (P) recipes have been marked as such. Additional recipes could be adapted so that they are suitable for vegetarians by simply swapping specific ingredients for an alternative.

PICNIC SUGGESTIONS

Here are a few suggestions for recipes that work well together. There's no need to follow a theme, but sometimes it can be fun. Obviously, pick and choose what works for you. If you like the mood of one of these menus, but would rather drop a few recipes and top up with store-bought goodies, then why not? Or agree to split the shopping and cooking between the picnic party to avoid taking on too much on your own.

Latin vibes

Watermelon Agua Fresca (page 139) and/or Passion Fruit, Coconut and Lime Batida (page 132)

Black Bean, Avocado, Kale and Quinoa Salad (page 38)

Prawn, Red Pepper and Chorizo Empanadas (page 64)

Corn and Jalapeño Muffins (page 31)

Passion Fruit and Coconut Slices (page 119)

Great for a crowd, Italian-style

Pea, Tarragon and Mascarpone Arancini (page 20)

Italo-Greek Picnic Pie (page 72)

Parma Ham and Buffalo Mozzarella with Spring Vegetables (page 42)

Tomato and Peach Panzanella with Honey, Smoked Salt and Lavender (page 49)

Grape, Lemon and Thyme Focaccia (page 124)

Peaches in Wine with Thyme Ricciarelli (page 128)

No-cook party

Rosé Sangria (page 140)

A Spanish Feast (page 24)

Watermelon and Feta Salad (page 50)

Prawn, Grapefruit and Green Apple Iceberg Cups (page 41)

Smoked Ham Sandwiches with Kimchi Slaw (page 99)

Wimbledon Buns (page 111)

A classy affair

Aioli and Friends (page 28)

Rebel Cucumber Sandwiches (page 104)

Crab Tart (page 76)

Gooseberry and Elderflower Traybake (page 108)

Tastes of the Levant

Walnut, Parsley and Sundried Tomato Babka (page 92)

Labneh, Dukkah, Salted Cucumber and Radishes (page 19)

Carrot, Cauliflower and Freekeh Salad (page 45)

Courgette, Chickpea and Feta Salad (page 37)

Harissa Chicken Sandwich (page 103)

Fig and Cherry Cardamom Friands (page 116)

Cakes and bubbly

Blueberry and Raspberry Loaf Cake (page 115)

Jam Lattice Tart (page 120)

Plum and Ricotta Pastries (page 112)

SIMPLE THINGS, SNACKS & DIPS

Food for sharing that you can leisurely pick on throughout the day is the backbone of a good picnic. Some of these dishes are portable picnic classics in their countries of origin. Others are quick recipes that bring together lovely ingredients with minimum effort.

3 GREAT DIPS

These dips are delicious eaten with flatbreads. They will keep in the fridge for up to 3 days, although the yoghurt dip is best on the day you make it.

Baba ganoush v

2 medium aubergines (eggplant)
1 tbsp tahini
juice of 1 large lemon
1 garlic clove, crushed
large pinch of ground cumin
1 tbsp chopped mint
light drizzle of extra virgin olive oil
sea salt, to taste

Spiced roasted carrot dip v

300g (10½oz) carrots, peeled and
    sliced into 2cm (¾in) rounds
1 onion, sliced
2 garlic cloves, peeled and halved
1 tsp cumin seeds
1 tsp pul biber chilli flakes
    or ¼ tsp crushed chillies
½ tsp ground coriander
2 tbsp extra virgin olive oil
3 tbsp Greek yoghurt
2 tbsp finely chopped coriander
    (cilantro)
sea salt, to taste

Yoghurt, cucumber and walnut dip v

100g (3½oz) small cucumbers
30g (1oz) walnut halves
300g (10½oz) Greek yoghurt
1 small garlic clove, crushed
1 tbsp finely chopped tarragon
¼ tsp dried mint
½ tsp dried dill
light drizzle of extra virgin olive oil
sea salt and freshly ground
    black pepper

> Serves 6–8
> –
> Prep 5 mins
> –
> Cook 40 mins

Baba ganoush

Keep the aubergines (eggplant) whole. If you have a gas hob, stove or barbecue, cook the aubergines directly over a high flame, turning them occasionally, until their skin is charred and crumbling and the flesh is soft and floppy. Cook for 15–30 minutes, depending on the size of your aubergines; your patience will be rewarded with a smoky, silky result.

Once cooled enough to handle, cut the aubergines in half, scoop out the flesh into a sieve (strainer) and leave to drain for 15 minutes. Discard the charred skin.

In a bowl, mash the aubergine flesh and stir in the remaining ingredients. Season with salt and add more lemon juice, to taste. Store in an airtight portable container in the fridge.

Spiced roasted carrot dip

Preheat the oven to 200°C (180°C fan)/400°F/gas 6. Put the carrots, onion and garlic in a small roasting tin (pan). Season with salt and stir in the spices and olive oil. Cover the roasting tin with foil, scrunching the sides to seal. Cook in the oven for 35–40 minutes or until the carrots are very soft.

Transfer the roasted carrots to a blender with the yoghurt and coriander (cilantro) and blitz until smooth. Store in an airtight portable container in the fridge.

Yoghurt, cucumber and walnut dip

Roughly peel the cucumbers, leaving some of the peel on. If using small Lebanese or pickling cucumbers, simply chop them finely; if using a large cucumber, halve it, scoop out the seeds and discard them before chopping.

Place the cucumber in a sieve and season with salt. Set aside to drain for 10 minutes. Meanwhile, toast the walnuts in a frying pan (skillet) over a low heat, shaking the pan regularly, until they start to char and smell nutty, about 3–4 minutes. Remove from the heat and, once cooled, roughly chop. Set aside.

Tip the seasoned cucumber into a bowl and stir in the yoghurt, garlic and herbs. Season with salt and pepper to taste, then transfer to an airtight portable container and keep chilled in the fridge. Just before leaving for your picnic, stir in the walnuts and a drizzle of olive oil.

QUINOA & SPINACH FRITTERS, WITH HERBED YOGHURT & TOMATO CHUTNEY v

Quinoa crisps up beautifully when pan-fried, giving these fritters a lovely crunch.

For the fritters
olive oil, for frying
150g (5½oz) baby leaf spinach
300g (10½oz) cooked quinoa
   (I use leftovers, a bought ready-
   cooked pouch, or I quickly boil
   150g (5½oz) raw quinoa to make
   300g (10½oz) when cooked)
2 spring onions (scallions),
   finely chopped
2 eggs, lightly beaten
2 garlic cloves, crushed
2 tbsp chopped coriander (cilantro)
grated zest of 1 unwaxed lemon
½ tsp sea salt
3 tbsp plain (all-purpose) flour
sea salt and freshly ground
   black pepper
tomato chutney, to serve

For the herbed yoghurt
250g (9oz) Greek yoghurt
2 tbsp roughly chopped mint
2 tbsp roughly chopped coriander
   (cilantro)
1 tbsp extra virgin olive oil

Heat 1 tbsp olive oil in a large pan over a medium heat, add the spinach, season with salt and cover with a lid. Turn the heat down to low and cook until the spinach wilts. Tip the spinach into a sieve (strainer) and set aside to cool and drain.

Squeeze any excess liquid out of the cooled spinach and chop it up roughly. Stir it into a large bowl with all the remaining fritter ingredients. Cover and chill for at least 30 minutes to allow the mixture to firm up (this could also be done a day ahead, if you prefer).

Heat a large frying pan (skillet) over a high heat and pour in enough oil to cover the base. When the oil is hot (the mixture should sizzle when it hits the hot oil), use a soup spoon to lower well-spaced spoonfuls of the quinoa mixture into the pan, flattening them slightly. Fry for 3–4 minutes on each side until golden and cooked through. Remove with a slotted spoon and transfer to a tray lined with kitchen paper. Repeat with the remaining mixture, adding more oil as needed.

Leave the fritters to cool completely before packing into a lidded container. Store at room temperature for up to 3 hours.

Meanwhile, make the herbed yoghurt by combining all the ingredients and seasoning to taste with salt and pepper. Pack into a jar or container with a tight-fitting lid and keep chilled until you leave for your picnic. Don't forget to pack some tomato chutney.

Makes 16
–
Prep 10 mins
–
Cook 30 mins
+ 30 mins
chilling

PRAWN & SESAME SCOTCH EGGS P

The beautiful lovechild of a scotch egg and sesame prawn toast, these are guaranteed crowd-pleasers!

6 eggs
400g (14oz) raw peeled prawns
(shrimp)
1 tbsp grated fresh ginger
6 spring onions (scallions),
finely chopped
2 garlic cloves, crushed
2 tbsp chopped coriander (cilantro)
2 tsp soy sauce
50g (1¾oz) cornflour (cornstarch)
60g (2¼oz) panko breadcrumbs
50g (1¾oz) sesame seeds
2 tsp milk
sunflower oil, for frying
chilli oil, to serve

First boil 4 of the eggs. Bring a pan of water to the boil, reduce the heat to a gentle simmer and delicately lower in 4 eggs. Cook for 6 minutes (for yolks that are still a little soft but not runny). Lift the eggs into a bowl of iced water and leave to cool completely.

Meanwhile, pat the prawns (shrimp) dry with kitchen paper. Transfer them to the bowl of a food processor and add the ginger, spring onions (scallions), garlic, coriander (cilantro) and soy sauce. Pulse to a coarse paste, then stir in 1 tbsp of the cornflour (cornstarch). Cover and chill for at least 30 minutes to allow the mixture to firm up.

Take three bowls: put the remaining cornflour in one, mix the breadcrumbs and sesame seeds together in the other, then crack the remaining 2 eggs into the third and beat in the milk. Peel the boiled eggs.

Divide the prawn mixture into 4 equal balls. Press one ball between 2 sheets of cling film (plastic wrap) and roll it out with a rolling pin (or press the mixture in the palms of your hands) until it is large enough to encase an egg. Peel off the top layer of cling film. Roll one of the boiled eggs in cornflour, then sit it in the middle of your rolled-out/pressed prawn mixture. Lift the bottom layer of cling film, using it to wrap the prawn mixture tightly and evenly around the egg. Remove the cling film and coat the encased egg in cornflour, then the beaten egg and lastly the breadcrumbs. Repeat with the remaining eggs.

To cook the scotch eggs, heat 10cm (4in) of oil in a wide heavy-based saucepan until a few breadcrumbs dropped into the hot oil turn golden after 10 seconds (or until the temperature reads 160°C (320°F) on a probe thermometer). Lower the eggs into the hot oil, and cook for 6–8 minutes, turning occasionally, until golden and crispy.

Remove with a slotted spoon, drain on kitchen paper and keep somewhere cool (or in the fridge if it's a very hot day), until packing for your picnic. I prefer to avoid putting the cooked eggs in the fridge, so I try to fry them no more than 2 hours before a picnic. Serve with chilli oil for dipping.

Makes 4
–
Prep 5 mins
–
Cook 20–25
mins + 30
mins chilling

LABNEH, DUKKAH, SALTED CUCUMBER & RADISHES v

Dukkah is an amazing flavour booster that can inject wonderfulness to pretty much anything it touches. Here I've scattered it over labneh, but the recipe makes more than you'll need, so store any leftovers in a jar to stir into salads, scatter over chicken before roasting, serve with olive oil and bread or simply snack on straight out of the jar when nobody's looking.

For the labneh
500g (1lb 2oz) Greek yoghurt
½ tsp salt
½ garlic clove, crushed

For the dukkah
100g (3½oz) almonds
   (I prefer to use unblanched)
50g (1¾oz) blanched hazelnuts
100g (3½oz) sesame seeds
100g (3½oz) pumpkin seeds
1 tsp olive oil
1 tbsp flaky sea salt
2 tbsp fennel seeds
2 tbsp coriander seeds
1 tbsp cumin seeds
1 tsp pink peppercorns

To serve
small Lebanese or pickling cucumbers
radishes, halved
extra virgin olive oil, to drizzle
flatbreads
sea salt, to taste

To make the labneh, mix the yoghurt, salt and garlic in a bowl until combined. Transfer the mixture to the centre of a clean piece of muslin (cheesecloth) or a couple of layers of thick kitchen paper, gather up the sides and twist to enclose the mixture. Place in a sieve (strainer) suspended over a large bowl and leave to drain in the fridge for at least 2 hours, or longer if you have the time, until thickened. Taste, adjusting the seasoning if needed. Transfer to an airtight container and keep chilled. It will keep in the fridge for up to 3 days.

To make the dukkah, preheat the oven to 200°C (180°C fan) /400°F/gas 6. Place the almonds, hazelnuts, sesame seeds and pumpkin seeds on a large baking sheet. Stir in the olive oil and salt and bake for 10 minutes. Stir in the remaining ingredients then return to the oven for another 10 minutes. Set aside and, once cooled, crush roughly in a pestle and mortar. Transfer to an airtight container and store for up to 2 weeks.

Just before leaving on your picnic, cut some cucumbers into large chunks and halve some radishes. Season both with salt and transfer to airtight portable containers. Serve the labneh with a drizzle of olive oil, a scattering of dukkah and the salted cucumber and radishes. You'll also want some fluffy flatbreads to mop it all up with.

Serves 4–6
–
Prep 5 mins
–
Cook 20 mins
+ draining

PEA, TARRAGON & MASCARPONE ARANCINI v

I love eating arancini as soon as they are fried, leaving them to cool just long enough to avoid burning my mouth. That will never be possible on a picnic, so I've found a way of ensuring that the rice stays soft and creamy even when cold. Out with the butter (which hardens when cold) and in with luscious mascarpone.

400ml (1¾ cups) vegetable stock
1 tbsp olive oil
1 onion, finely chopped
125g (4½oz) risotto rice
3 tbsp dry vermouth or dry white wine
60g (2¼oz) frozen peas, defrosted
2 tbsp chopped tarragon
2 tbsp mascarpone
3 tbsp freshly grated Parmesan cheese
75g (2½oz) plain (all-purpose) flour
75g (2½oz) panko breadcrumbs
1 egg
1 tsp milk
sunflower oil, for frying
sea salt and freshly ground
    black pepper
lemon wedges, to serve

Bring the stock to the boil in a saucepan, then lower the heat to a slow simmer.

Heat the olive oil in a heavy-based saucepan over a low heat and gently cook the onions for 10 minutes until softened.

Add the rice to the softened onions and cook, stirring, for 1 minute. Pour in the vermouth or wine and cook, stirring, until all the liquid has been absorbed. Add 2 ladles of simmering stock to the rice. Stir continuously until the stock has been absorbed and the rice parts when a wooden spoon is run through it. Add another ladleful of stock and continue stirring and adding stock in stages until the rice is creamy and tender to the bite, about 16–18 minutes.

Stir in the peas, tarragon, mascarpone and grated Parmesan and taste, seasoning as needed. Leave to cool completely.

Wet your hands and take 1 tbsp of risotto and roll to form a ball about the size of a golf ball. Repeat with the remaining rice to make 25 balls.

Take three bowls: put the plain (all-purpose) flour in one, the breadcrumbs in another, then crack the egg into the third and beat in the milk. Roll each ball in flour, then dip into the beaten egg/milk and coat in the breadcrumbs. The arancini can be prepared to this stage up to 1 day before you plan to eat them; cover with cling film (plastic wrap) and store in the fridge. Fry them on the morning of your picnic.

To fry the arancini, heat 5cm (2in) of oil in a wide saucepan until a few breadcrumbs dropped into the hot oil turn golden after 10 seconds (or until the temperature reads 160°C/320°F on a probe thermometer). Lower the arancini in batches into the oil and cook for 6–8 minutes or until golden and crispy.

Drain on kitchen paper and keep uncovered, somewhere cool for up to 3 hours until packing for your picnic. Remember to also pack lemon wedges to squeeze over the top of the arancini just before eating.

Makes 25
–
Prep 10 mins
–
Cook 1–1¼ hours

PLOUGHMAN'S LUNCH

You can have the most amazing ploughman's lunch without even stepping into the kitchen – a great deli will have you covered. I like to mix up store-bought and homemade bits, such as these confit shallots, sweetened with sticky dates and balanced with the sharp citrus of lemon. It works beautifully with the sweetness of the ham and the richness of the cheese. Not quite traditional, but you can always pack a jar of piccalilli and Branston Pickle, and avoid cooking entirely, if you prefer.

Shop for

thick-sliced ham: you'll need
    a couple of slices per person
red apples: something crisp and
    sharp like a Braeburn or McIntosh
a mature, crumbly Cheddar,
    Lancashire or Manchego
brown (whole wheat) sourdough
gherkins
English (yellow) mustard
salted butter

For the shallot, lemon and date confit

1 lemon
6 banana shallots, halved
    lengthways and peeled
4 Medjool dates, pitted
    and halved
2 garlic cloves, skin on
1 red chilli
a few thyme sprigs
extra virgin olive oil

For the confit shallots, preheat the oven to 170°C (150°C fan) /325°F/gas 3. Cut the lemon into 4 long wedges, then cut each wedge into 0.5cm (¼in) triangle-shaped slices. Place the shallots cut-side-up in a small ovenproof dish with the lemon slices and remaining solid ingredients; they should fit snugly.

Pour in enough olive oil to submerge all the ingredients. Cover with foil and transfer to the oven. Cook for 1 hour, or until the shallots are soft. Spoon into a jar using a slotted spoon, then save any oil left behind in a separate jar. It makes a great dressing for grain salads, and I love to add it to Puy (French) lentils as an instant flavour boost.

Pack all the elements of the ploughman's lunch separately and unpack onto a large platter or board once you've chosen your picnic spot.

Prep 5 mins
–
Cook
1 hour

A SPANISH
FEAST

This Spanish spread is all about careful shopping and minimal cooking. You could opt out of cooking altogether, but this Romesco Sauce is irresistible. If you don't have time to make it, there is no shame in grabbing a tub from a deli or supermarket. I find it impossible to give quantities but be sure to pack some Spanish serrano or *pata negra* ham, juicy tomatoes, crusty bread, Spanish or Portuguese anchovies in olive oil and olives or caperberries.

Shop for
a few garlic cloves
white sourdough, toasted if you like
a few juicy, ripe tomatoes
anchovies in olive oil
caperberries or olives
extra virgin olive oil
flaky sea salt
romesco sauce (if not
    making the recipe below)
serrano or *pata negra* ham

For the romesco sauce
45g (1½oz) almonds (I prefer
    to use unblanched)
30g (1oz) blanched hazelnuts
1 tbsp extra virgin olive oil,
    plus extra for drizzling
20g (¾oz) fresh breadcrumbs
1 tsp sweet smoked paprika
2 garlic cloves, chopped
100g (3½oz) roasted red peppers,
    from a jar
1 tbsp sherry vinegar
sea salt and freshly ground
    black pepper

For the romesco sauce, toast the almonds and hazelnuts in a dry frying pan (skillet) over a low heat until golden, about 5 minutes. Tip into a food processor and blitz until finely chopped but not ground. Transfer to a bowl. Don't wash the food processor – you'll need it again in a minute.

Return the pan to a medium heat. Pour in the olive oil and, once hot, add the breadcrumbs, paprika and garlic. Fry, stirring until the breadcrumbs are golden, then tip the mixture into the food processor. Add the red peppers and vinegar and blitz until almost smooth. Stir this mixture into the chopped nuts and taste, seasoning with salt and pepper and adjusting the quantity of vinegar and olive oil until it tastes right to you. Pack in a sealed container and keep chilled until needed.

To serve, unpack all your lovely produce onto serving boards. Make *pan con tomate*: rub a garlic clove over the top of some of the sourdough slices, then either cut the tomatoes in half and run them up and down the bread, smashing them as you go, or grate the tomatoes and spoon the flesh over the slices (the coarse side of a box grater is perfect for this). Enjoy the breads topped with a drizzle of olive oil and sprinkling of sea salt, or top with anchovies or ham. Top the remaining bread slices with romesco, or romesco and ham also works well. Pick and choose your preferred combinations and enjoy.

Prep 5 mins
–
Cook
10 mins

CLASSIC SCOTCH EGGS

The quintessential British picnic snack. I like to keep my egg yolks a little runny, which means the shelled eggs will be quite soft, and may be tricky to handle when putting the scotch eggs together – but I hope you'll agree it's worth the extra effort.

6 eggs
1 tbsp olive oil
400g (14oz) good-quality sausage meat
1½ tbsp English (yellow) mustard
1 tbsp chopped flat-leaf parsley
1 tbsp chopped thyme
50g (1¾oz) plain (all-purpose) flour
100g (3½oz) dried breadcrumbs
2 tsp milk
sunflower oil, for frying
sea salt and freshly ground
    black pepper

To serve
Piccalilli, English mustard or ketchup

First boil 4 of the eggs. Bring a pan of water to the boil, reduce the heat to a gentle simmer and delicately lower in 4 eggs. Cook for 6 minutes for yolks that are still a little runny. Lift the eggs into a bowl of iced water and leave to cool completely.

Meanwhile, put the sausage meat, mustard and herbs in a large bowl. Season with salt and pepper, then mix well with your hands and divide the mixture into 4 equal balls.

Take three bowls: put the plain (all-purpose) flour in one, the breadcrumbs in another, then crack the remaining 2 eggs into the third bowl and beat in the milk. Peel the boiled eggs.

Squash a sausage meat ball between 2 sheets of cling film (plastic wrap) and roll out with a rolling pin, or squash with the palm of your hand until it is large enough to encase an egg. Peel off the top layer of cling film. Roll one of the boiled eggs in the flour, then sit it in the middle of your rolled-out sausage meat. Lift the cling film, wrapping the sausage meat around the egg, and use your hands to mould the meat tightly and evenly around the egg. Remove the cling film and coat the scotch egg in flour, then the beaten egg/milk and lastly the breadcrumbs. Repeat with the remaining eggs.

To cook the scotch eggs, heat 10cm (4in) of oil in a wide saucepan, until a few breadcrumbs dropped into the hot oil turn golden after 10 seconds (or until the temperature reads 160°C/320°F on a probe thermometer). Lower the eggs into the oil and cook for 8–10 minutes, turning until golden and crispy. Drain on kitchen paper and keep, uncovered, in a cool place. I prefer to avoid having to put them in the fridge, so I try to fry my scotch eggs no more than 2 hours before a picnic.

Makes 4
–
Prep 5 mins
–
Cook
20 mins

AIOLI & FRIENDS v

I can't decide whether this combination screams English country garden or springtime in Provence. Either way, it's definitely somewhere I want to be. The smoked salt is not essential, but I highly recommend it, and if you're looking for more ways of using it, the Tomato and Peach Panzanella (see page 49), would be a great place to start.

400g (14oz) asparagus, woody ends snapped off
12 quail eggs (or 4–6 eggs, boiled for 6 minutes)
2 heads Little Gem lettuce, leaves separated
sea salt and freshly ground black pepper
smoked flaky sea salt, to serve

For the aioli
2 egg yolks
2 tsp Dijon mustard
1 large garlic clove, crushed
juice of ½ lemon
350ml (1½ cups) olive oil (not extra virgin)

First make the aioli. Combine the egg yolks, mustard, garlic and lemon juice in a bowl using a small whisk. Slowly whisk in the oil, a little at a time, until you have a mayonnaise consistency. If the aioli is getting too thick, add 2 tsp warm water before whisking in the remaining oil. Season with salt and pepper to taste and store in a sealed container in the fridge.

Cook the asparagus and quail eggs in a pan of salted boiling water – the eggs will need 2 minutes, and the asparagus will need 2–4 minutes depending on its thickness. Drain and refresh in iced water. Drain again and pack in separate containers (no need to shell the eggs). The aioli will keep in the fridge for up to 2 days.

Serve the asparagus, quail eggs and lettuce leaves on a large platter, with the aioli and smoked salt on the side for dipping and sprinkling (peeling the eggs first, of course).

Simple Things, Snacks & Dips

Serves 4–6
–
Prep 5 mins
–
Cook 10 mins

CORN & JALAPEÑO MUFFINS WITH MAPLE BUTTER v

These are delicious eaten just as they are as a snack, or bake them to take as the bread element to accompany a larger picnic.

For the muffins
65g (2¼oz) unsalted butter,
    plus extra for greasing
1 small red onion, finely chopped
125g (4½oz) sweetcorn (corn)
    kernels (fresh or canned)
1 green jalapeño chilli, ½ chopped,
    ½ sliced into rounds
2 eggs
180g (6¼oz) Greek yoghurt
180ml (6¼oz) whole milk
130g (4½oz) cornmeal or polenta
100g (3½oz) plain (all-purpose) flour
½ tsp sea salt
2 tsp baking powder
3 tbsp chopped coriander (cilantro)
40g (1½oz) mature Cheddar, grated
2 spring onions (scallions), thinly sliced

For the maple butter
2 tbsp maple syrup
100g (3½oz) unsalted butter,
    slightly softened

Butter the holes of a 12-hole muffin tin (pan) and set aside.

Melt 15g (½oz) of the butter in a pan over a low heat. Add the onion, cook for 5 minutes, then stir in the sweetcorn (corn) and chopped jalapeño and cook for a further 5 minutes until lightly golden and soft. Tip the mixture into a large bowl to cool, then add the remaining butter to the hot pan and leave it to melt off the heat.

Crack the eggs into the cooled sweetcorn mixture and mix with a fork, then stir in the yoghurt, milk and cooled melted butter. Next combine the cornmeal or polenta in a bowl with the plain (all-purpose) flour, salt and baking powder, then add the dry mixture to the bowl with the wet mixture and gently combine. Finally add the coriander (cilantro), Cheddar and spring onions (scallions) and mix well.

Spoon the mixture into the prepared muffin holes and top with the sliced jalapeño rounds. Bake for 20–25 minutes, until golden and a skewer inserted into the centre comes out clean. Leave to cool in the tray for 5 minutes, then move to a wire rack to cool completely before packing for the picnic.

The muffins are best eaten on the day of baking. The mixture can be made and spooned into the tray the day before and kept chilled until baking, in which case add 2 minutes to the cooking time.

For the maple butter, beat the maple syrup into the softened butter and transfer to a container. I like to use a dariole mould or ramekin, then cover it using a piece of baking paper secured with a rubber band. Keep chilled in the fridge until you head out.

Makes 12
–
Prep 10 mins
–
Cook 35 mins

SALADS

The perfect picnic salad is one that improves with time, benefitting from sitting at room temperature, soaking in its dressing and letting the flavours mingle. That's why grains, pulses, potatoes, tomatoes and robust salad leaves with crunch are picnic heroes.

ORANGE & FENNEL SALAD VE

This Sicilian salad can be prepared ahead of time – or, if you're planning to pick up the ingredients on the way to your picnic spot, make sure to pack a chopping board and a knife so you can throw it together outdoors.

1 large fennel bulb
12 black olives unpitted
  (or pitted if you prefer)
3 tbsp extra virgin olive oil
large pinch of crushed
  red chilli flakes
2 oranges
sea salt

Thinly slice the fennel and toss it, together with its fronds, into a dish with the olives and oil. Season with salt and the crushed chilli flakes.

Using a serrated knife, cut away the skin and pith of the oranges and slice the fruit thinly into rounds. Add the orange slices, along with any juice, to the fennel salad and toss very gently to combine.

Serves 4
–
Prep
10 mins

COURGETTE, CHICKPEA & FETA SALAD v

This salad is delicious warm as a light dinner, or at room temperature when on a picnic. The beauty of it is that the flavours get better the longer it sits. I like to eat it with some peppery wild rocket leaves, served on the side (keeping it separate stops the leaves wilting on the way to the picnic).

5 tbsp olive oil
2 courgettes (zucchini), cut into chunks
zest of ¼ unwaxed lemon, sliced into thin strips
2 red onions, thinly sliced
2 garlic cloves, thinly sliced
1 red chilli, sliced into rounds
½ tsp coriander seeds
1 tsp cumin seeds
2 × 400g (14oz) cans chickpeas (garbanzos), drained and rinsed
3 tbsp sherry vinegar (it sounds like a lot, but it works!)
200g (7oz) feta cheese (vegetarian, if you prefer), diced
1 handful coriander (cilantro) leaves, torn
1 handful mint leaves, torn
sea salt and freshly ground black pepper
100g (3½oz) wild rocket (optional), to serve

Heat 2 tbsp of the olive oil in a large frying pan (skillet) over a medium-high heat. Add the courgette (zucchini), season with salt and pepper and cook until the courgette is just starting to soften and colour, about 3 minutes. Add the lemon zest and cook for 1 minute more until the aroma of the lemon comes through, then tip the contents of the pan into a large bowl.

Return the pan to the heat and add the remaining 3 tbsp olive oil, the onions, garlic and chilli, giving everything a good stir. Roughly crush the coriander and cumin seeds in a pestle and mortar, then stir them into the pan. Cook for 1 minute, then add the chickpeas (garbanzos), season with salt and cook, stirring regularly, until the onions have softened, about 10 minutes (reduce the heat if it's starting to catch and burn).

Pour in the vinegar and cook for a further 2 minutes or so, until the liquid has evaporated. Remove from the heat and gently fold the oniony chickpea mixture into the courgettes. Season with salt and pepper to taste, then set aside to cool.

Once at room temperature, gently toss the feta and herbs into the salad and transfer to the container you will be taking it to the picnic in. The salad will keep well in the fridge for up to 2 days. Pack a bag of rocket in your cool bag, to add to the salad before serving.

Serves 4
–
Prep 15 mins
–
Cook 25 mins

BLACK BEAN, AVOCADO, KALE & QUINOA SALAD WITH CORIANDER DRESSING v

This salad might read like a parody of the wellness-obsessed noughties, with its quinoa, kale and avocados. Well, this one has stood the test of time, not least for its punchy lime-sharp dressing, which I would happily drink out of the jar (just don't call it a green juice!). Also, because there is no risk of it wilting, kale is the perfect leaf for picnic salads – a bit of sitting around in a dressing to tenderize it is exactly what it needs.

100g (3½oz) quinoa
½ tsp sweet paprika
5 tbsp extra virgin olive oil
3 corn tortillas
400g (14oz) can black turtle beans, drained and rinsed
½ small red onion, thinly sliced
200g (7¾oz) cherry tomatoes, halved
juice of 1 lime
150g (5½oz) kale, trimmed of thick stalks and roughly chopped
2 avocados
sea salt and freshly ground black pepper

For the coriander dressing
25g (1oz) coriander (cilantro), including stalks
1 large garlic clove
grated zest and juice of 1 unwaxed lime
3 tbsp sour cream
1 green chilli

Preheat the oven to 200°C (180°C fan)/400°F/gas 6.

Rinse the quinoa then put it in a medium saucepan. Pour in 200ml (scant 1 cup) water, season with salt and bring to the boil. Cover with a tight-fitting lid and cook over a low heat for 12–15 minutes until tender. Tip into a large bowl and set aside to cool.

Meanwhile, to make the tortilla crisps, put the paprika and 3 tbsp of the olive oil in a large bowl and stir to combine. Lightly brush the oil over both sides of the tortillas, then cut the tortillas into triangles. Arrange in a single layer on a baking sheet and bake for 8–10 minutes until golden. They might feel a bit soft, but will crisp up once cooled. Sprinkle with salt and set aside to cool.

While the tortilla chips are baking, toss the beans, red onion and cherry tomatoes into the cooled quinoa and pour in any remaining paprika-flavoured olive oil. Add the lime juice, pour in the remaining 2 tbsp olive oil and season with salt and pepper. Add the kale, then toss well to combine, and keep in the fridge until you are ready to go out (it will keep for up to 6 hours).

Make the dressing by whizzing all the ingredients in a food processor, then season with salt to taste.

When packing for your picnic, keep the avocados, salad, dressing and tortilla crisps separate. Once you're ready to eat, slice the avocados onto the salad. Drizzle generously with the dressing, then serve with the tortilla crisps and any remaining dressing on the side.

Serves 4
–
Prep 10 mins
–
Cook 25 mins

PRAWN, GRAPEFRUIT & GREEN APPLE ICEBERG CUPS WITH COCONUT DRESSING P

This is such a gorgeous refreshing salad. You could, of course, toss all the ingredients together, which would probably make it much more practical to transport, but where would be the fun in that?

1 pink grapefruit
1 Granny Smith apple,
    cut into matchsticks
1 red chilli, chopped
1 banana shallot, thinly sliced
300g (10½oz) cooked shelled
    king prawns (shrimp)
handful coriander (cilantro) leaves
handful mint leaves
handful Thai basil leaves
1 iceberg lettuce
3 tbsp toasted peanuts, crushed
    in a pestle and mortar
crispy fried onions (the
    store-bought kind)

For the coconut dressing
4 tbsp coconut milk
1 tbsp fish sauce
1 tsp caster (superfine) sugar

Peel and segment the grapefruit over a large bowl to collect any juices, placing the segments on a plate. Stir the dressing ingredients into the bowl with the grapefruit juices, mix to combine, then gently stir through the grapefruit segments, apple, chilli, shallot and prawns (shrimp). Cover and keep chilled (it will keep for up to 2 hours at this stage).

Just before heading out on your picnic, toss the herbs into the salad and transfer to a sealed container. Pack the iceberg, peanuts and fried onions each in their own container.

To serve, let everyone make their own cups: take a lettuce leaf, spoon in the prawn salad, then top with a sprinkling each of crushed peanuts and fried onions. Scrunch up the leaf lightly to partially close it and enjoy, trying your best not to spill any.

Serves 4
–
Prep 25 mins
–
No cook

Salads

PARMA HAM & BUFFALO MOZZARELLA WITH SPRING VEGETABLES

Salty Parma ham with sweet, milky buffalo mozzarella is a marriage made in heaven. Add to that some simply dressed spring vegetables and you have a sunny, light picnic salad.

250g (9oz) asparagus spears
100g (3½oz) fresh or frozen peas
100g (3½oz) fresh or frozen broad (fava) beans
3 tbsp extra virgin olive oil, plus extra to drizzle
1 unwaxed lemon
2 tbsp roughly chopped tarragon
2 buffalo mozzarella balls
8 slices Parma ham
sea salt and freshly ground black pepper
crusty bread, to serve

Snap the woody ends off the asparagus and discard them. Cook the asparagus in a pan of salted boiling water for 1 minute, then add the peas and broad (fava) beans and cook for a further 2 minutes. Drain and refresh under cold running water.

Tip the blanched vegetables into a large bowl and toss through the olive oil, the grated zest of ½ lemon and the tarragon. Season with salt and pepper to taste and transfer to an airtight container. Keep chilled until you leave for your picnic; the salad can be prepared to this stage quite a few hours ahead, but I wouldn't leave it overnight.

To serve, transfer the dressed vegetables to a large platter. Use your hands to tear the buffalo mozzarella and plate it next to the vegetables, draping the ham next to it. Drizzle the dish with olive oil, a squeeze of lemon juice and add a sprinkling of salt and pepper. Enjoy with some crusty bread.

Serves 4–6
–
Prep 5 mins
–
Cook 10 mins

CARROT, CAULIFLOWER & FREEKEH SALAD VE

You can use any grain for this salad if you don't have freekeh: barley, spelt or bulgur wheat would all give the same nutty bite. If you're in a hurry, you could blitz the carrots and cauliflower in a food processor until roughly chopped, but I find the salad looks much prettier when chopped by hand.

100g (3½oz) cracked freekeh
2 carrots, peeled and thinly sliced
(any shape you find easiest is fine)
250g (9oz) cauliflower, cut into
florets and very thinly sliced
1 small red onion, halved and
thinly sliced
40g (1½oz) mixed fresh herbs
(I like a combination of mint,
dill and parsley), stalks discarded
and leaves roughly chopped
150g (5½oz) pomegranate seeds
sea salt and freshly ground
black pepper

For the dressing
5 tbsp extra virgin olive oil
juice of ½ lemon
1 tsp ground cumin
½ tsp ground cinnamon
1 large garlic clove, crushed
sea salt, to taste

Heat a frying pan (skillet) over a medium-high heat. Add the freekeh and toast the grains, turning them frequently in the dry pan until fragrant, about 2 minutes. Tip the grains into a pan of salted boiling water and boil for 15–20 minutes until al dente. Drain and refresh under cold running water to stop it cooking any further.

Toss the cooled freekeh into a large bowl with the carrots, cauliflower, onion, herbs and pomegranate seeds. In a separate bowl, whisk together all the dressing ingredients, adding salt to taste, and an extra squeeze of lemon juice if you think it needs it. Thoroughly toss the dressing through the salad, then taste and adjust the seasoning if needed.

Keep the salad in an airtight portable container in the fridge until you're ready to head out. It will keep well in the fridge for up to 2 days.

Serves 6
–
Prep 15 mins
–
Cook 25 mins

Salads

GIANT COUSCOUS SALAD WITH SAFFRON-ROASTED TOMATOES & BEETROOT v

This salad is deliciously rich and generous, with earthy, punchy flavours. I serve it with Greek yoghurt and harissa on the side, or pair it with the Labneh, Dukkah, Salted Cucumber and Radishes (see page 19) and perhaps a couple of the 3 Great Dips (see page 12).

600g (1lb 5oz) medium tomatoes, halved
400g (14oz) smallish raw beetroot (beets), cut into thin wedges
3 garlic cloves, sliced
1 red chilli, finely sliced
large pinch of saffron strands
5 tbsp extra virgin olive oil
2 tbsp honey
200g (7oz) giant wholemeal (whole wheat) couscous
1 preserved lemon, halved, inner flesh discarded and rind thinly sliced (if you can't find preserved lemons, finely grate an unwaxed lemon and season the zest with salt before using instead)
20g (¾oz) dill, roughly chopped
½ lemon
sea salt and freshly ground black pepper

To serve
Greek yoghurt
harissa

Preheat the oven to 200°C (180°C fan)/400°F/gas 6. Put the tomatoes and beetroot (beet) in a roasting tin (pan) into which they fit comfortably in a single layer. Add the garlic and chilli, then sprinkle in the saffron strands, breaking them between your fingers as you go. Drizzle in 2 tbsp of the olive oil, the honey, season with salt and pepper and toss well to combine.

Rearrange the tomatoes, making sure they are all sitting cut-side-up, and roast for 40–45 minutes, or until the beetroot is tender and the tomatoes are looking gorgeously rich and soft. Set aside to cool. Don't worry if the beetroot still has a little bite; it will carry on cooking in its own heat as it cools.

Meanwhile, tip the couscous into a medium pan and toast it over a medium-high heat for 2–3 minutes, stirring, until it begins to colour. Add 400ml (1¾ cups) water, season with salt and bring to the boil. Cover with a lid, reduce the heat to low and cook for 10 minutes until the water has been absorbed. Give the couscous a good stir, cover again and set aside off the heat for 10 minutes for the couscous to steam in its own heat.

Transfer the couscous to a large bowl and stir in the preserved lemon rind, remaining 3 tbsp olive oil and half the dill. Squeeze in the juice of the ½ lemon. Toss well to make sure the couscous is well coated and taste, adjusting the seasoning if it needs it. Cover and keep chilled; it will keep for up to 1 day at this stage.

Just before heading out for your picnic, spoon the saffron-roasted vegetables and their juices over the couscous and scatter with the remaining dill. Enjoy with a dollop of Greek yoghurt and some harissa on the side.

Serves 4–6
–
Prep 20 mins
–
Cook 45 mins

TOMATO & PEACH PANZANELLA WITH HONEY, SMOKED SALT & LAVENDER v

This is the easiest of recipes, but I break the prep into three parts: first, I season the tomatoes, giving the smoky salt a chance to get right into them; second, 30 minutes to 2 hours before the picnic, I toss in the onions, dressing and toasted sourdough to give the bread a chance to soak up the juices; finally, I top the salad with peach wedges and a flourish of lavender and honey, just before tucking in.

800g (1lb 12oz) ripe tomatoes, in a variety of shapes, colours and sizes
flaky smoked salt, to taste
3 tbsp extra virgin olive oil
1½ tbsp red wine vinegar
½ red onion, thinly sliced
2 thick slices day-old sourdough bread
2 ripe peaches, cut into wedges
a few lavender flowers (optional)
good-quality honey (I like to use a lavender or wildflower honey)

Slice the tomatoes, or cut them into halves, quarters or wedges, depending to their shape and size. Put them in a large bowl and season generously with smoked salt. Cover and set aside for at least 30 minutes (longer is fine).

30 minutes to 2 hours before you plan on eating, toss the olive oil, vinegar and red onion into the tomatoes. Toast the bread until well charred and, once cooled, break large chunks into the salad. Toss well to combine, then transfer the salad to an airtight container and keep chilled until you go out.

Just before eating, add the peach wedges and scatter with the lavender flowers (if using), breaking the flowers slightly between your fingers as you go. Toss the salad well to combine, then drizzle over some honey; about 2 tsp should do it.

Serves 4
–
Prep 5 mins
–
Cook 5 mins
+ 30 mins
sitting

Salads

WATERMELON & FETA SALAD WITH MINT & SHALLOT DRESSING v

I love the sweet, salty and sour sun-kissed kick this salad delivers. You'll want all the flavours to stay fresh and distinct, so only bring them together at the last minute. The only prep I do at home is to make the dressing and chill the watermelon, which I take with me whole, to keep it cool and juicy.

1 small watermelon, well chilled
200g (7¾oz) feta cheese (vegetarian,
   if you prefer)
small handful mint leaves

For the shallot dressing
1 banana shallot, thinly sliced
1 tbsp red wine vinegar
2 tbsp olive oil
1 tbsp honey
sea salt and freshly ground
   black pepper

To make the dressing, mix the shallot, vinegar, olive oil and honey in a jar or sealed container. Season with salt and pepper and seal well.

Once at the picnic, cut the watermelon open. Scoop the flesh of the watermelon onto a serving platter. Add the feta, broken into large chunks, and spoon over the shallot dressing. Scatter with mint leaves before serving.

Serves 4
–
Prep 2–3 mins
–
No cook

VIETNAMESE
-ISH CHICKEN
SLAW

Sometimes, the healthiest of salads can also be the tastiest. For a more substantial salad, toss in some vermicelli rice noodles.

3 skinless chicken breasts
2cm (¾in) piece fresh ginger, sliced
15g (½oz) each Thai basil, mint and
    coriander (cilantro), leaves picked
    and set aside, stalks reserved
3 tbsp sesame seeds
2 tbsp rice vinegar
4 tbsp fish sauce
1 tbsp caster (superfine) sugar
juice of 2 limes
1 red chilli, deseeded and
    finely chopped
2 carrots, cut into matchsticks
¼ red cabbage, core removed
    and finely shredded
100g (3½oz) bean sprouts
3 spring onions (scallions), shredded

First poach the chicken. Put the chicken, ginger and reserved herb stalks in a small pan and pour in enough water to cover. Bring to the boil over a high heat. Reduce the heat to a slow simmer and cook for 10 minutes. Remove from the heat, cover and set aside until completely cooled, by which time the chicken will be cooked through.

Meanwhile, toast the sesame seeds in a frying pan (skillet) over a low heat until golden, then tip them into a large bowl. Stir in the vinegar, fish sauce, sugar, lime juice and chilli. Add the carrots, red cabbage, bean sprouts and spring onions (scallions), then shred in the cooled chicken. Toss everything well to combine, cover and chill in a sealable container in the fridge, for up to 2 days.

Just before heading out, toss in the herb leaves.

CRUSHED ROASTED POTATO & SALSA VERDE SALAD P

Give this a try if (like me) you are not a fan of potato salads made with mayo. I love serving it with the Porchetta Sandwiches (see page 100) and Apricot Frangipane Galette (see page 123), as a Sunday roast picnic.

1kg (2lb 4oz) medium new potatoes
large pinch of crushed red chillies
2 tbsp olive oil
sea salt

For the salsa verde
1 tbsp salted capers, rinsed,
   squeezed dry and chopped
2 anchovy fillets, chopped
2 garlic cloves, finely chopped
25g (1oz) bunch flat-leaf parsley,
   leaves only, chopped
25g (1oz) bunch mint, leaves only,
   chopped
grated zest of 1 unwaxed lemon
3 tbsp extra virgin olive oil
1 tbsp red wine vinegar
2 tsp Dijon mustard

Preheat the oven to 200°C (180°C fan)/400°F/gas 6. Cook the potatoes in a pan of salted boiling water for 20–25 minutes until cooked through. Drain well.

Tip the potatoes into a large roasting tin (pan) and use the back of a fork (or the heel of your hand if the potatoes are cool enough) to gently push down on the potatoes, crushing them slightly without breaking them apart completely. Season with salt, scatter with crushed chillies, then drizzle with the 2 tbsp olive oil. Roast for 40–45 minutes, turning halfway through cooking, until golden and crispy.

Meanwhile, combine all the ingredients for the salsa verde. I like to keep mine quite chunky, to keep the flavour of separate ingredients distinct, but you can chop finely, or even whizz in a food processor, if you prefer.

Transfer the roasted potatoes to a large bowl and toss through the salsa verde. Do this while the potatoes are still warm, so they soak in all the flavours of the dressing. Set aside to cool before packing. Ideally, make the salad on the day of your picnic, so it keeps its crunch, but it can also be made a day ahead and chilled in the fridge, in which case take it out of the fridge in time for it to come to room temperature before eating.

Serves 4–6
–
Prep 5 mins
–
Cook 1 hour
15 mins

TARTS, PIES & FRITTATAS

Tarts and pies are picnic classics. Empanadas, sausage rolls and my asparagus tartlets are easy to pass around, and are my pick where kids are involved. The larger tarts that call for careful serving are for gentler picnics where they can be eaten calmly off a precariously balanced plate. And frittatas? They're crowd-pleasers at any occasion.

TRADITIONAL SAUSAGE ROLL

Sausage rolls make the perfect picnic food: easy to pack, equally delicious warm or cold – and you don't even need plates or cutlery. Oh, and they're delicious! No wonder they're a British picnic staple.

1 tbsp olive oil
1 red onion, finely chopped
1 tsp fennel seeds
5 sage leaves
30g (1oz) fresh breadcrumbs
1 tbsp Dijon mustard
400g (14oz) good-quality sausage meat
1 × 320g (11¼oz) sheet ready-rolled puff
    pastry, defrosted if frozen
plain (all-purpose) flour, for dusting
1 egg, lightly beaten
2 tsp sesame seeds
1 tsp nigella seeds
sea salt and freshly ground
    black pepper

Preheat the oven to 200°C (180°C fan)/400°F/gas 6.

To make the filling, heat the olive oil in a frying pan (skillet) over a low heat. Add the chopped onion, fennel seeds and sage leaves and season. Cook for 10 minutes, stirring occasionally, until softened. Tip the cooked onions into a large bowl and, once they have completely cooled, stir in the breadcrumbs, mustard and sausage meat. Mix well to combine.

Unroll the pastry sheet onto a lightly floured surface. Cut the pastry in half lengthways to make 2 long lengths. Divide the sausage meat mixture in half and shape into 2 long cylinders, placing them just off-centre along each piece of pastry. Brush one edge of the pastry with some of the beaten egg. Fold the pastry over the sausage meat mixture to fully enclose, pressing the pastry edges together to seal. Turn the sausage rolls over so they are seam-side-down and use a serrated knife to cut each into thirds to make 6 sausage rolls.

Transfer the rolls to a baking sheet lined with baking paper. Brush the top and sides with the remaining beaten egg and sprinkle evenly with sesame and nigella seeds. Bake for 35–40 minutes, until golden and cooked through. Cool completely on a wire rack before wrapping them to take on the picnic.

Makes 6
–
Prep 5 mins
–
Cook 55–60 mins

TOMATO & ROMESCO TART v

People often ask me how a recipe writer creates new recipes. This time, it was mostly luck. My plan had been to make a ricotta and tomato tart, but I forgot to buy the ricotta. I scoured the fridge for ideas and, luckily, found the romesco made the day before for the Spanish Feast (see page 24). And so, my favourite recipe in this book was born.

For the pastry
170g (6oz) unsalted butter, cubed and well chilled
250g (9oz) plain (all-purpose) flour, plus extra for dusting
large pinch of salt
2 tsp honey
4 tbsp chilled water

For the topping
400g (14oz) ripe baby plum tomatoes, halved
1 tbsp olive oil, plus extra for brushing
1 tsp honey
150g (5½oz) Romesco Sauce (half of the recipe from Spanish Feast, see page 24)
4 tbsp coarsely grated Manchego (or flavourful vegetarian hard cheese)
few thyme sprigs, leaves picked (optional)
sea salt and freshly ground black pepper

For the pastry, pulse the butter, flour and salt in the bowl of a food processor until the mixture resembles breadcrumbs. Add the honey and water and whizz until the pastry comes together, adding an extra 1–2 tsp water if needed. Bring the pastry together into a ball, wrap in cling film (plastic wrap) and chill for 30 minutes.

Meanwhile, put the tomatoes in a colander and season them with salt. Set aside over a bowl to drain for 30 minutes to 1 hour. The salt will season the tomatoes and also draw out some of their moisture.

Once the tomatoes have had their time, give them a good shake over the sink to let the juices drain out, then tip them into a large bowl and gently stir through the olive oil and honey.

Preheat the oven to 190°C (170°C fan)/375°F/gas 5, positioning a baking sheet in the middle of the oven to heat. Roll the pastry out onto a large piece of baking paper dusted with flour – you're aiming for a rough rectangle about 30cm x 25 cm (12in x 10in) and 0.5cm (¼in) thick. Carefully move the baking paper with the pastry onto a second baking sheet. Spread the centre of the pastry with romesco, leaving a 5cm (2in) border, then arrange the tomatoes, cut-side-up over the top. Fold the pastry border over the tart to partly enclose the tomatoes, letting the pastry overlap where this happens naturally.

Brush the pastry edge of the tart with olive oil and scatter the cheese all around the border. Take the heated baking sheet out of the oven and carefully slide the tart, with the baking paper it's sitting on, onto the hot baking sheet.

Bake for 45–50 minutes until the pastry is crisp and golden, covering the top with foil if it starts to take on too much colour. Cool on the baking sheet over a wire rack and scatter with fresh thyme leaves before packing for your picnic.

Serves 4–6
–
Prep 15 mins
+ draining
–
Cook 40–45 mins

HERBED COURGETTE & NEW POTATO FRITTATA v

The trick to a great frittata is to make sure that all the vegetables are cooked until they are really tasty before stirring them into the egg mixture, so take your time with the onions, potatoes and courgettes (zucchini) and taste first to check their seasoning before adding the eggs.

3 tbsp olive oil
1 large onion, thinly sliced
500g (1lb 2oz) medium new potatoes,
    sliced about 0.5cm (¼in) thick
300g (10½oz) courgette (zucchini),
    cut in half lengthways, then into
    1cm (½in) semi-circles
6 medium eggs, lightly beaten
20g (¾oz) dill, finely chopped
20g (¾oz) flat-leaf parsley,
    leaves only, chopped
sea salt and freshly ground
    black pepper

Heat 2 tbsp of the oil in a heavy-based, ovenproof, non-stick 20–22cm (8–8½in) frying pan (skillet) with a lid. Stir in the onions and potatoes and season with salt and pepper. Cook, covered, over a low heat for 15–20 minutes or so, stirring occasionally, until the potatoes are cooked and the onions translucent and tender.

Transfer to a large bowl and return the pan to the hob, increasing the heat to high. Heat ½ tbsp of the remaining oil, add the courgettes (zucchini) and season. Cook for 2 minutes or so on each side to give them a little colour. Tip the courgettes into the bowl with the potatoes and onions.

In a large measuring jug, mix together the beaten eggs and herbs. Season, then add the egg mixture to the bowl with the cooked vegetables and stir well.

Preheat the grill (broiler) until very hot.

Return the frying pan to a medium heat and add the remaining ½ tbsp olive oil. When the oil is hot, pour in the frittata mixture and quickly arrange the vegetables so that they're evenly dispersed. Turn the heat to low, cover and cook for 10–12 minutes or until all but the top of the frittata is set.

Finish the cooking under the preheated grill, about 10cm (4in) from the heat source. Cook until lightly coloured. Give the pan a shake to loosen the frittata, then transfer to a plate to cool.

The frittata will keep in the fridge for 2 days. To pack, wrap the whole frittata in baking paper, or first cut it into wedges and wrap individually, if you find that easier.

Serves 6–8
–
Prep 10 mins
–
Cook 40 mins

PRAWN,
RED PEPPER
& CHORIZO
EMPANADAS

These tasty empanadas are really easy to make. The twisted seal might seem fiddly at first, but with a little practice it becomes child's play. If you want to hone your technique, there are some brilliant videos online by Argentinian home cooks showing how it's done.

For the pastry
300g (10½oz) plain (all-purpose) flour, plus extra to dust
1 tsp salt
110g (3¾oz) unsalted butter, cubed and well chilled
1 egg, plus 1 lightly beaten egg for glazing
4 tbsp chilled water
1 tsp white vinegar

For the filling
75g (2½oz) cooking chorizo, finely chopped
1 small onion, finely chopped
75g (2½oz) potatoes, peeled and cut into pea-sized pieces
125g (4½oz) raw shelled prawns (shrimp), chopped
45g (1½oz) roasted peppers from a jar, chopped
1 tbsp chopped flat-leaf parsley

To make the pastry, put the flour, salt and butter in a food processor and pulse to a fine breadcrumb consistency. Add the egg and pulse to combine, then add the water and vinegar, bit by bit, until the pastry is just starting to come together, adding a little extra chilled water if it is still too crumbly. Turn out, press the mixture together, wrap in cling film (plastic wrap) and refrigerate for 30 minutes.

For the filling, cook the chorizo in a medium frying pan (skillet) with a lid over a medium-low heat for 2–3 minutes until starting to crisp up. Use a slotted spoon to transfer the chorizo to a plate, leaving the rendered fat in the pan over the heat. Stir in the onions and potatoes and season with salt and pepper.

Cook, covered, over a low heat for 15 minutes or so, stirring occasionally, until the potatoes are cooked and the onions translucent and really tender. Stir in the chopped prawns and as soon as they turn pink, remove the pan from the heat and add the peppers and parsley. Set aside to cool.

Preheat the oven to 200°C (180°C fan)/400°F/gas 6 and line two baking sheets with baking paper. To shape the empanadas, divide the dough into 12 equal pieces and cover them with a clean dish towel. On a floured work surface, roll 1 pastry round into a 12cm (4½in) circle.

Spoon 2 tsp of the filling into the centre of the dough circle and fold in half to make a semi-circle-shaped parcel. Press the edges together firmly then twist your way around to crimp the edge; or, if you prefer, simply press the edges together using the tines of a fork. Transfer to a baking sheet and continue shaping the remaining dough balls and filling in the same way, until you have 12 parcels. The empanadas can now be covered and chilled in the fridge for up to 1 day before baking, if you like.

To bake, brush the empanadas with beaten egg and bake for 25–30 minutes until golden. Switch the position of the oven trays 20 minutes into cooking to give the empanadas a chance to brown evenly. Cool on a wire rack. The empanadas keep well at room temperature for one day.

Makes 12
–
Prep 15 mins
+ chilling time
–
Cook 50 mins
–1 hour

ASPARAGUS & GRUYÈRE TARTLETS v

These are so quick to make, especially if you buy ready-rolled pastry. The recipe makes 4 tartlets, which would serve 2 people if you're not serving much else. If you're eating them as part of a larger spread, 1 tart per person will be plenty.

1 × 320g (11¼oz) sheet ready-rolled
   puff pastry, defrosted if frozen
4 tbsp crème fraîche
1 tbsp Dijon mustard
1 garlic clove, crushed
1 tbsp chopped tarragon
50g (1¾oz) gruyère, grated (or
   flavourful vegetarian hard cheese)
400g (14oz) asparagus
1 tbsp olive oil
1 egg, lightly beaten with a fork
sea salt and freshly ground
   black pepper

Preheat the oven to 200°C (180°C fan)/400°F/gas 6.

Unroll the puff pastry onto a baking tray (sheet pan) and cut it into 4 equal rectangles.

In a bowl, combine the crème fraîche, Dijon, garlic, tarragon and gruyère. Season with black pepper (no need for salt – there's enough in the cheese). Spread the gruyère mixture over the pastry rectangles, leaving a 2cm (¾in) border.

Snap the woody ends off the asparagus and discard them. Put the asparagus in a bowl and drizzle over the olive oil. Season, toss well to coat the spears in the oil, then divide them evenly between the tartlets. Brush the pastry border with the beaten egg and bake for 20–25 minutes, until golden and cooked through.

Cool on the tray over a cooling rack. Wait until the tarts are completely cooled before packing them for your picnic.

Makes 4
–
Prep 10 mins
–
Cook 25 mins

LEEK & STILTON QUICHE WITH WALNUT PASTRY v

Unashamedly old-fashioned flavours that are still deliciously comforting: guaranteed to entice any quiche sceptics out there.

For the pastry

200g (7oz) plain (all-purpose) flour, plus extra to dust
50g (1¾oz) shelled walnuts, whizzed in a food processor until finely ground
75g (2½oz) salted butter, cubed and well chilled
1 egg yolk
1 tbsp chilled water

For the filling

2 eggs, plus 2 egg yolks
30g (1oz) unsalted butter
500g (1lb 2oz) leeks, cut into 1cm (½in) rounds
120g (4¼oz) Stilton or other blue cheese such as Oxford Blue
50ml (3½ tbsp) whole milk
150ml (scant ⅔ cup) double (heavy) cream
sea salt and freshly ground black pepper

For the pastry, blitz the flour, ground walnuts and butter in a food processor until the mixture resembles breadcrumbs. Add the egg yolk and chilled water and pulse until the pastry comes together into a ball. Add a little extra water if the pastry is still too crumbly. Wrap in cling film (plastic wrap) and chill for 30 minutes.

Preheat the oven to 200°C (180°C fan)/400°F/gas 6. Roll the chilled pastry out on a floured surface and use to line a 20cm (8in) loose-bottomed cake tin (pan), trimming off any excess. This pastry can be quite crumbly to work with, so if it breaks, simply patch up any holes or cracks with extra pastry. Chill in the fridge for 15 minutes.

Prick the base of the pastry case all over with a fork, then line with baking paper, fill with ceramic baking beans/pie weights (rice or dry pulses also work) and cook the pastry for 15 minutes. Remove from the oven, tip out the baking beans and discard the paper.

Break the eggs for the filling into a large jug (pitcher) and lightly beat with a fork. Lightly brush the base of the pastry case with a little of the beaten egg and return to the oven for 5–7 minutes for the pastry to get some colour and to seal the base. Set aside. Reduce the oven to 180°C (160°C fan)/350°F/gas 4.

Meanwhile start making the filling. Melt the butter in a large frying pan (skillet) with a lid over a low heat. Add the leeks and 1 tbsp water. Season with salt and pepper and cook, covered, for 10–15 minutes, stirring occasionally, until the leeks are tender.

Spoon the leeks into the pastry case, making sure they're evenly distributed, then crumble in the Stilton.

Use a wooden spoon to stir the milk and double (heavy) cream into the jug with the eggs. Season, then slowly pour the mixture into the pastry case. Bake for 35–40 minutes or until the top is golden and the filling is just set in the middle (a slight wobble is good). Leave to cool on a wire rack.

I like to keep the tart in the tin to make it easier to transport. The tart will keep for 1 day at room temperature.

Serves 8–10
–
Prep 20 mins
+ chilling time
–
Cook 1 hour
10 mins

INDIVIDUAL ARTICHOKE & POTATO GALETTES v

These galettes are so delicious. The trick is to buy the best jarred artichokes you can get your hands on and cook the potatoes using the oil from the jar. The rich, buttery artichoke flavour will seep into the potatoes, making them irresistible.

For the pastry
150g (5½oz) wholemeal (whole wheat) or white spelt flour
150g (5½oz) plain (all-purpose) flour, plus extra for dusting
200g (7oz) salted butter, cubed and well chilled
1 egg
1 tbsp chilled water

For the filling
160g (5¾oz) grilled (roasted) artichokes in olive oil (drained weight), drained and cut into wedges; keep the oil
15g (½oz) salted butter
800g (1lb 12oz) new potatoes, sliced about 1cm (½in) thick
4 tbsp Greek yoghurt
1 garlic clove, crushed
2 tbsp chopped mint, plus extra mint leaves, to serve
1 egg, lightly beaten
sea salt and freshly ground black pepper

For the pastry, put the flours and cubed butter in the bowl of a food processor and pulse until the mixture resembles breadcrumbs. Crack in the egg, add the chilled water and pulse until the pastry comes together into a ball. Add a little extra water if the pastry is still too crumbly. Wrap in cling film (plastic wrap) and chill for 30 minutes.

Meanwhile, start the filling. Spoon 2 tbsp of the olive oil from the artichokes into a large lidded frying pan (skillet) over a medium heat. Add the butter and, once melted, toss in the potatoes and artichokes. Season with salt and pepper, cover with the lid and cook for 10 minutes, occasionally giving everything a stir. At this stage the potatoes won't be quite cooked all the way through, but that's fine as they'll finish cooking in the oven. Allow the filling to cool.

Preheat the oven to 200°C (180°C fan)/400°F/gas 6. Combine the yoghurt, garlic and chopped mint in a small bowl and season.

Divide the chilled pastry into four even-sized balls and roll out on a floured work surface into four approximately 0.5cm (¼in) thick rounds. Spread the yoghurt mixture over the rounds, leaving a 2.5cm (1in) border. Top evenly with the cooled potato and artichokes, then fold the pastry border over to enclose some of the filling. Repeat with the remaining galettes. Transfer the galettes to a baking sheet lined with baking paper and brush the pastry borders with the beaten egg. Bake for 30–35 minutes until the pastry is crisp and golden.

Cool on a wire rack before packing. Scatter with fresh mint leaves to serve.

Makes 4
—
Prep 25 mins + chilling
—
Cook 40–45 mins

ITALO-GREEK PICNIC PIE v

If it's a centrepiece you're after for your picnic, then this is the pie for you. It's my version of an Italian recipe, but I've added a bit of Greece to it with a salty kick of feta and some sweet-earthy caraway.

For the pastry
250g (9oz) plain (all-purpose) flour, plus extra for dusting
2 tbsp caster (superfine) sugar
pinch of salt
100g (3½oz) unsalted butter, cubed and well chilled
½ tsp caraway seeds, plus extra for sprinkling
2 egg yolks, plus 1 beaten egg for glazing
2–3 tbsp whole milk

For the filling
400g (14oz) new potatoes, sliced into rounds
2 tbsp olive oil
2 garlic cloves, bruised with the side of a knife
300g (10½oz) spinach
150g (5½oz) feta cheese (vegetarian, if you prefer), crumbled
200g (7oz) ricotta
3 eggs
4 spring onions (scallions), finely sliced into rounds
40g (1½oz) mixed fresh herbs (I use mint, dill and basil)
sea salt and freshly ground black pepper

For the pastry, tip the flour, sugar and salt into the bowl of a food processor and pulse to combine. Add the butter and caraway seeds and pulse until the mixture resembles coarse breadcrumbs. Add the egg yolks and 2 tbsp milk and pulse until the dough comes together. If it's still too crumbly, add another 1 tbsp milk, in stages, until the dough comes together. Tip out of the mixer and shape into two discs, one slightly larger than the other. Wrap in cling film (plastic wrap) and chill for 1 hour until firm.

While the pastry is chilling, put the potato slices in a large wide-based pan (use one with a tight-fitting lid). Drizzle in the olive oil and place over a medium heat. Add the garlic cloves, season with salt and pepper, cover with the lid and cook for 15–20 minutes, occasionally giving everything a stir, until the potatoes are tender and starting to break apart.

Scoop the garlic cloves out of the pan and discard, then tip the spinach into the pan, over the potatoes, cover with the lid and leave the spinach to wilt for a few minutes. Give the potatoes and spinach a stir and, once the spinach is fully wilted, remove the pan from the heat and leave to cool.

Preheat the oven to 180°C (160°C fan)/350°F/gas 4.

In a large bowl, use a wooden spoon to beat together the feta and ricotta. Season to taste, then beat in the eggs, spring onions (scallions) and chopped herbs. Fold through the spinach and potatoes.

On a lightly floured worktop, roll out the larger pastry disc to a 0.5cm (¼in) thickness and use to line a 20cm (8in) springform cake tin (pan). Fill the pastry case with the spinach and potato mixture. Brush the edges of the pastry with some of the beaten egg.

Roll out the remaining pastry to the same thickness and cover the pie, pressing down the edges. Trim away excess pastry with a knife and crimp the edges with your fingers. Make a small cross-shaped incision into the centre of the pastry for the steam to escape during baking. Brush with the remaining beaten egg, then sprinkle with caraway seeds.

Bake for 40–45 minutes, covering the top with foil if it starts browning too much. Cool the pie on a wire rack before removing from the tin. Enjoy warm or at room temperature.

Serves 10–12
–
Prep 10 mins
+ chilling
–
Cook 1 hour
40 mins

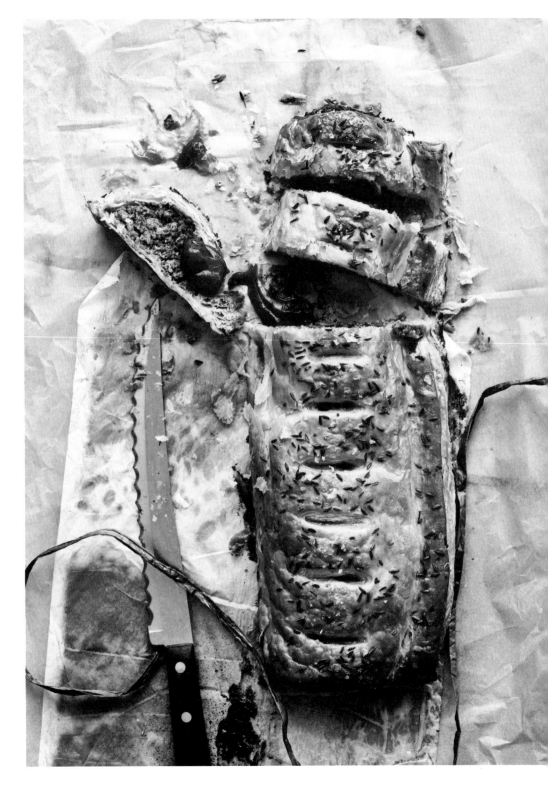

SONALI'S GIANT LAMB KEEMA ROLL

My lovely friend Sonali was my right-hand angel on the days we shot the pictures you see in this book. A food stylist and chef, Sonali has a real talent for layering flavours and making food that people want to eat, so I was over the moon when she let me use her recipe for Lamb Keema Roll. She usually makes it as small party bites, but we thought it might be fun to turn it into a giant picnic roll.

1 red onion, quartered
3 fat garlic cloves
2–3 green chillies
400g (14oz) minced (ground) lamb
2 tsp tomato paste
½ tsp ground turmeric
1 tsp ground cumin
½ tsp ground coriander
2 tsp garam masala
1 tsp salt
1 × 320g (11¼oz) sheet ready-rolled
    puff pastry, defrosted if frozen
1 egg, beaten
1–2 tsp cumin seeds

Preheat the oven to 200°C (180°C fan)/400°F/gas 6. Put the red onion, garlic and chillies in the bowl of a food processor and blitz until very finely chopped. Transfer to a large bowl, add the lamb, tomato paste, all the spices and the salt. Mix well with your hands, squeezing as you go to bring the meat together – this is your keema mix.

Line a large baking tray (sheet pan) with baking paper. Carefully unroll the puff pastry sheet onto the baking paper. Using your hands, shape the keema mixture into a long sausage shape, placing it just off-centre along the length of the pastry. Brush the edges with some of the beaten egg, then fold the pastry over the meat to fully enclose. Use a fork to seal the pastry edges together.

Brush the top of the pastry with the remaining beaten egg, sprinkle over the cumin seeds, then gently score the top of the roll at regular intervals using the tip of a sharp knife. Bake for 35–40 minutes until golden and cooked through. Cool completely on a wire rack before wrapping to take on your picnic.

Serves 10–12
–
Prep 15 mins
–
Cook 35–40 mins

CRAB TART P

Crabmeat always feels like such a treat to me and I almost prefer the rich umami kick you get from brown meat to the delicate sweet white flakes. This recipe uses both, but if you prefer a more subtle crab flavour, stick to only white meat.

For the pastry
150g (5½oz) wholemeal (whole wheat) or white spelt flour
100g (3½oz) plain (all-purpose) flour, plus extra for dusting
150g (5½oz) unsalted butter, cubed and well chilled
1 egg yolk

For the filling
2 eggs, plus 2 egg yolks
2 tsp olive oil
1 small onion, finely chopped
70g (2½oz) crème fraîche
150ml (5fl oz) double (heavy) cream
½ tsp English (yellow) mustard powder
50g (1¾oz) brown crabmeat
200g (7oz) white crabmeat
sea salt and freshly ground black pepper
watercress, to serve

For the pastry, blitz the two types of flour and the butter in a food processor until the mixture resembles breadcrumbs. Add the egg yolk and ½ tbsp chilled water and pulse until the pastry comes together into a ball. Add a little extra water if the pastry is still too crumbly. Wrap in cling film (plastic wrap) and chill for 30 minutes.

Preheat the oven to 200°C (180°C fan)/400°F/gas 6. Roll the pastry out on a floured surface and use to line a 23cm (9in) loose-bottomed cake tin (pan). Chill in the fridge for 15 minutes.

Prick the base of the pastry case all over with a fork, then line with baking paper and ceramic baking beans/pie weights (rice or dry pulses also work), and cook the pastry for 15 minutes. Remove from the oven, tip out the baking beans and remove the paper.

Crack the eggs for the filling into a large jug (pitcher) and lightly beat with a fork. Lightly brush the base of the pastry case with a little of the beaten egg and return to the oven for 5–7 minutes for the pastry to get some colour and to seal the base. Set aside. Reduce the oven temperature to 180°C (160°C fan)/350°F/gas 4.

Meanwhile, heat the oil in a small frying pan (skillet) over a low heat. Add the onions, season with salt and pepper and cook for 8–10 minutes until softened.

Use a wooden spoon to mix the crème fraîche, double (heavy) cream and mustard into the jug with the eggs. Season well then stir in the softened onions and crab meats. Slowly pour into the pastry case and bake for 25–30 minutes or until the top is lightly golden and the filling is just set in the middle (a slight wobble is good). Leave to cool on a wire rack.

I like to keep the tart in the tin, to make it easier to transport. Serve with a scattering of watercress.

The tart will keep for 1 day at room temperature.

Serves 10–12
–
Prep 20 mins
+ chilling time
–
Cook 45 mins

ROASTED SQUASH & ONION FRITTATA v

Squash, red onion and coriander (cilantro) are one of my favourite flavour combinations, making this my go-to frittata.

500g (1lb 2oz) squash or pumpkin,
   peeled and cut into 2.5cm (1in)
   wedges (or diced)
1 large red onion, cut into thin wedges
3 tbsp olive oil
6 eggs
2 tbsp plain yoghurt
25g (1oz) coriander (cilantro),
   stalks finely chopped and leaves
   roughly chopped separately
1 garlic clove, crushed
½ red chilli, thinly sliced into rounds
sea salt and freshly ground
   black pepper

Preheat the oven to 200°C (180°C fan)/400°F/gas 6. Put the squash and red onion in a roasting tin (pan) into which they fit comfortably in a single layer. Drizzle with 2 tbsp of the olive oil and season with salt and pepper. Roast for 30–35 minutes until tender and browning at the edges. Transfer to a large bowl and taste to check the seasoning.

In a large measuring jug, beat together the eggs, yoghurt and chopped coriander (cilantro) leaves. Season and set aside.

Heat ½ tbsp of the remaining olive oil in a heavy-based, ovenproof, non-stick 20–22cm (8–8½in) frying pan (skillet) over a medium heat. Add the chopped coriander stalks, garlic and chilli and fry for 30 seconds or until their aroma is released. Add this mixture to the bowl with the cooked vegetables, then pour in the egg mixture and quickly stir to combine.

Preheat the grill (broiler) until very hot.

Return the frying pan to a medium heat and add the remaining ½ tbsp olive oil. When the oil is hot, pour in the frittata mixture and quickly arrange the vegetables so that they're evenly dispersed. Turn the heat to low, cover and cook for 10–12 minutes or until all but the top of the frittata is set. Finish the cooking under the preheated grill, about 10cm (4in) from the heat source. Cook until lightly coloured. Give the pan a shake to loosen the frittata, then transfer to a plate to cool.

The frittata will keep in the fridge for 2 days. To pack, wrap the whole frittata in baking paper, or first cut it into wedges and wrap individually, if you find that easier.

Serves 6–8
–
Prep 10 mins
–
Cook 50–55 mins

ANNIE'S MINI PORK PIES

When developing this recipe I called my friend, pie queen Annie Rigg, who immediately sent me her book *Pies & Tarts*. Annie's original recipe makes 1 larger pie, but I've adapted it here to make little individual ones. The messy crimping you see here is all mine, but the beautiful pastry and tasty filling is 100% Annie magic.

For the filling
400g (14oz) lean pork shoulder
200g (7oz) rindless (skinless) and boneless pork belly
150g (5½oz) rindless smoked streaky bacon (sliced smoked bacon)
1 Bramley apple, cored, peeled and finely diced
60g (2¼oz) cooked chestnuts, finely diced
½ tbsp chopped fresh sage
1 tsp fresh thyme leaves
light grating of nutmeg
½ tsp cayenne pepper
½ tsp English (yellow) mustard powder
I fat garlic clove, minced
1 tbsp chopped flat-leaf parsley
sea salt and freshly ground black pepper

For the hot water crust pastry
300g (10½oz) plain (all-purpose) flour, plus a little extra for dusting
250g (9oz) strong white flour
½ tsp caster (superfine) sugar
good pinch of sea salt flakes, crushed
pinch of freshly ground black pepper
150g (5½oz) lard, diced
50g (1¾oz) unsalted butter, diced, plus extra for greasing
200ml (scant 1 cup) water
2 medium eggs, beaten

Makes 12
–
Prep 30–35 mins + cooling
–
Cook 1 hour 15 mins

Cut the pork shoulder, belly and bacon into 0.5cm (¼in) dice and mix well. Put two thirds of the meat into the bowl of a food processor and pulse until minced – you may need to do this in batches. Mix the diced and minced pork together in a bowl. Add the remaining filling ingredients, season well and mix to combine. Cover and chill until needed.

For the pastry, mix the flours, sugar and salt and black pepper in a large bowl and make a well in the centre. Put the lard, butter and water in a small pan set over a medium heat. Allow the lard and butter to melt into the water, increase the heat and bring to the boil. Roughly mix three quarters of the beaten egg into the well in the centre of the seasoned flour, add the hot water mixture and, working quickly, mix the dough together until smooth. Cover with a clean dish towel and set aside for 20 minutes until just cool enough to handle.

Preheat the oven to 180°C (160°C fan)/350°F/gas 4. Grease the holes of a 12-hole muffin tin (pan) with butter. Lightly dust the work surface with flour.

Cut off about two thirds of the pastry, leaving the other third under the dish towel to keep it warm. Roll the larger piece out to a thickness of about 3mm (⅛in). With a cookie cutter, cut out twelve 11cm (4¼in) circles and line the holes of the muffin tin, making sure that the pastry covers the base and sides of the holes, and that the top of the pastry just overhangs.

Pack the filling mixture into the pastry, mounding it up slightly in the middle. Roll out the remaining pastry and cut into twelve 8cm (3¼in) circles for the lids. Brush the edges of the pastry with water and lay the lids on top, pressing the edges together to seal. Trim off the excess pastry and crimp the edges of the pies between your fingers. Brush the tops of the pies with the remaining beaten egg. Use a skewer to make a hole in the top of each pastry lid for steam to escape.

Bake the pies for 45 minutes to 1 hour. They should be a deep golden colour and the filling cooked through after this time.

Remove the pies from the oven and allow to cool, then chill overnight before taking on your picnic and serving with brown sauce, mustard and pickles.

SANDWICHES & BREADS

Flavoured breads are my go-to for picnics – they're like sandwiches that don't need filling, and look and taste way more impressive than the skill it takes to make them. And you'll find the sandwiches picnic-proof: most can handle sitting around for a bit without going soggy, and some actively benefit from doing so, giving the bread time to soak in the beautiful juices.

PLAIN FOCACCIA VE

Growing up in Rome, my favourite sandwich was pizza bianca with mortadella. You'd show the guy behind the counter what size sandwich you were after, then he'd fill the bread with enough wafer-thin mortadella slices to feed a small village. This plain focaccia is a slightly thicker version, which I find more foolproof to make. For a thinner bread, more akin to pizza bianca, use a slightly larger tin.

500g (1lb 2oz) strong white bread flour
7g (2¼ tsp) fast-action yeast
    or 14g (½oz) fresh yeast
350ml (1½ cups) lukewarm water
1 tsp caster (superfine) sugar
10g (¼oz) salt, plus extra for
    the topping
1 tbsp extra virgin olive oil, plus
    extra for drizzling, greasing
    and topping
mortadella, to serve (optional)

The day before baking, combine the flour, yeast, water, and sugar in a large bowl. Work the mixture together with a spatula, or your hands, to form a soft dough with no pockets of flour. Cover with a large plate or dish towel and set aside for 30 minutes. Sprinkle in the salt and the 1 tbsp of olive oil and use your hands to work them into the dough.

Grease a separate large bowl with another 1 tbsp olive oil and use a dough scraper or a spatula to help you transfer the dough to the oiled bowl. Drizzle a little more olive oil over the top of the dough, spreading it to lightly coat the surface. Cover and set aside for 1 hour, then transfer to the fridge to chill overnight, or for up to 2 days (I often make 2 batches in one day, to bake on consecutive days).

Take the dough out of the fridge about 3 hours before you want to bake it. Let it come to room temperature for 2 hours. Line a baking tray (sheet pan) that measures approximately 20cm x 30cm (8in x 12in) with baking paper. Pour a little olive oil over the baking paper and spread it around with the palm of your hands to make sure the paper is well greased. Slide the dough onto the paper and gently stretch the dough to cover the paper. Leave to prove for 1–1½ hours, on a cool day. It will look fluffy and full of air bubbles when it's ready.

Preheat the oven to 220°C (200°C fan)/425°F/gas 7, with a shelf positioned in the centre of the oven.

Once the dough has proved, make a brine by combining 1 tbsp each of olive oil and water with a large pinch of salt. Dip your fingertips into this brine and press them along the dough to give it dimples. Drizzle the rest of the brine all over the dough.

Bake the dough in the preheated oven, on the middle shelf, for 20–25 minutes, until golden.

Serves 8–10
-
Prep 5 mins
+ overnight
chilling, resting
and proving
-
Cook 25 mins

RED ONION, OLIVE & CHILLI FOCACCIA v

I don't think I've ever made exactly the same focaccia twice. The topping varies depending on what I have to hand: jarred artichokes, sliced new potatoes, cherry tomatoes. This topping is great when you're serving it as part of a spread: it's flavoursome enough to stand alone, but not so topping-heavy that it can't be served as bread to accompany salads or cheese.

Focaccia dough (see page 84)

For the topping
3 tbsp olive oil
2 garlic cloves, sliced
2 large sprigs rosemary, leaves removed from the main stalk
2 red chillies, sliced into rounds
2 large red onions, cut into thin wedges
handful of pitted black olives
flaky sea salt

The day before you plan to bake this focaccia, follow the method for the Plain Focaccia recipe on page 84 up to the point where the dough has proved and you have made the dimples on the surface with your fingertips and poured the brine over it.

Preheat the oven to 200°C (180°C fan)/400°F/gas 6 with a shelf positioned in the centre of the oven.

For the topping, pour 2 tbsp of the olive oil into a small bowl and stir in the garlic, rosemary and chillies. Set aside.

In a separate bowl, gently toss the onions and olives with the remaining olive oil until well coated. Top the focaccia with the onions and olives, then add a final sprinkle of flaky salt.

Bake the focaccia in the preheated oven, on the heated shelf, for 25 minutes. Evenly spoon over the rosemary and garlic oil and return the tray to the oven, turning it around so that the focaccia bakes evenly. Bake for a further 10–15 minutes, until golden. Cool on a wire rack.

The focaccia is best eaten on the day it is baked but will keep in an airtight container for up to 2 days.

Serves 8–10
–
Prep 15 mins
+ overnight chilling, resting and proving
–
Cook 40 mins

Sandwiches & Breads

RED PEPPER & HARISSA BUNS v

Cute, easy to pack and a total crowd-pleaser. My kids like heat, but when they were younger I used to leave out the harissa or replace it with a little tomato passata.

For the dough

675g (1lb 8oz) plain (all-purpose) flour, plus extra for kneading
2 tsp instant yeast
1½ tsp salt
75g (2½oz) unsalted butter, plus extra for greasing
350ml (1½ cups) whole milk
2 tbsp Greek yoghurt
1 egg, lightly beaten

For the filling and glaze

2 large garlic cloves, crushed
2 tbsp harissa
3 tbsp olive oil
400g (14oz) roasted red peppers (drained weight, if from a jar), cut into long strips about 2.5cm (1in) wide
4 tsp za'atar
1 tbsp honey

For the dough, combine the flour, yeast and salt in a large bowl. In a small pan, gently warm the butter and milk until the butter has melted and the milk is lukewarm. Remove from the heat, then quickly stir in the yoghurt and egg and, once well combined, pour into the bowl with the dry mixture. Mix to form a sticky dough. Cover the bowl and leave to rise for 1 hour (or overnight in the fridge, then let it come to room temperature for 30 minutes before shaping), until light and fluffy.

Meanwhile, butter a 12-hole muffin tin (pan). For the filling, combine the garlic, harissa and 2 tbsp of the olive oil in a small bowl and set aside.

Knead the risen dough on a floured worktop for a few seconds to knock out excess air then use a rolling pin to roll it out to a rectangle about 30cm x 45cm (12in x 18in). Spoon on the harissa mixture, using the back of the spoon or a pastry brush to spread it evenly over the whole surface. Top with the peppers, aiming to cover the surface evenly, but not worrying too much about making a neat job of it, then scatter with half the za'atar.

Starting at one of the longer edges of the dough, roll the dough up tightly like a Swiss (jelly) roll, then, using a large knife, slice it into 12 buns. I find the easiest way to do this is to cut it first in half, then cut each in half again, then cut each quarter into 3 equal slices. Sit the buns, cut-side-up, in the holes of the prepared muffin tin.

Don't worry if some of the buns lose their shape or even fall apart a bit; once baked, they'll hold together, and a loose rustic look suits them. Cover with a dish towel and set aside to prove for 1 hour. Meanwhile, preheat the oven to 200°C (180°C fan)/400°F/gas 6.

Combine the honey and the remaining za'atar and 1 tbsp olive oil in a small bowl and use to brush the top of the buns. Bake for 20–22 minutes or until cooked through. Cool in the tin before packing for your picnic.

These are best eaten on the day of baking, but will keep in an airtight container for up to 2 days.

Makes 12
–
Prep 20 mins
+ proving
–
Cook 22 mins

CHEESY COURGETTE SCONES ᵥ

Get the baking just right and these scones rise to be deep and proud, with a lovely moist crumb. Undercook them slightly and they might deflate as they cool, making them look less triumphant, but possibly even more delicious in texture, with an irresistible gooeyness. Either way, it's a win.

225g (8oz) self-raising flour,
  plus extra for dusting
½ tsp salt
1 tsp English (yellow) mustard powder
½ tsp cayenne pepper
75g (2½oz) chilled unsalted butter
1 medium courgette (zucchini),
  coarsely grated
50g (1¾oz) mature Cheddar, coarsely
  grated, plus 25g (1oz) extra for
  sprinkling
100ml (3½fl oz) buttermilk,
  plus extra for glazing
1 tsp caraway seeds, for sprinkling

Preheat the oven to 200°C (180°C fan)/400°F/gas 6. Line a baking sheet with baking paper. Combine the flour, salt, mustard and cayenne pepper in a large bowl. Coarsely grate the butter and stir it through the flour, then use your fingertips to gently rub the butter into the flour for a few seconds (work quickly to prevent the butter from melting from the heat from your hands).

Use a large metal spoon to fold the courgette (zucchini) and the Cheddar into the bowl, then fold in the buttermilk until just combined. Don't worry if you are left with a few little pockets of flour.

Tip out onto a lightly floured surface and knead briefly, just enough to bring the mixture together, and form into a 20cm (8in) circle. Cut into 8 equal wedges and transfer the wedges to the lined baking sheet. Chill in the freezer for 15 minutes or in the fridge for 40 minutes.

Brush the top of each scone with a little buttermilk and sprinkle with the extra Cheddar and the caraway seeds. Bake for 25–30 minutes, or until golden and cooked through.

Cool on a wire rack before packing. These scones are great eaten as they are, or with butter or Marmite. They are best eaten the day you bake them, but they will keep well in an airtight container for up to 2 days.

Makes 8
–
Prep 20 mins
–
Cook 25–30
mins

WALNUT, PARSLEY & SUNDRIED TOMATO BABKA v

This recipe is easier than it might seem. If you've never made a babka, find a video tutorial online to give you confidence. Or, shape and bake it into rolls like the ones on page 89.

For the dough

350g (12oz) strong white bread flour, plus extra for dusting
7g (2¼ tsp) instant yeast
220ml (7½fl oz) tepid water
2 tsp runny honey
1 tsp salt, plus extra to scatter on top
olive oil, for greasing and brushing

For the filling

40g (1½oz) walnuts, finely chopped
15g (½oz) parsley leaves, finely chopped
40g (1½oz) sun-blush tomatoes, chopped into small pieces
2 garlic cloves, crushed
½ tsp fennel seeds
3 tbsp olive oil

Line a 1.2 litre (40fl oz), about 20cm x 10cm (8in x 4in) loaf tin (pan) with baking paper.

Combine the flour, yeast, water and honey in a large bowl. Work the mixture together with a spatula or your hands to form a soft dough with no pockets of flour. Cover with a large plate or dish towel and set aside for 30 minutes. Sprinkle in the salt and use your hands to work it into the dough.

Turn onto a lightly floured surface and knead for 10 minutes until elastic. Place in a lightly oiled bowl, cover and leave to rise in a warm place for 1½ hours, or until doubled in size.

Meanwhile, combine all the ingredients for the filling and set aside.

Gently tip the dough onto a work surface. Roll it out to a rectangle about 20cm x 30cm (8in x 12in). Spread the filling over the surface of the dough. Starting with a long edge, tightly roll the rectangle to make a long log and lay it seam-side-down on the work surface.

Using a large sharp knife, cut the dough lengthways down the centre, leaving the halves attached at one end by about 3cm (1¼in). Lift the left length over the right length, then continue to twist the 2 lengths around each other until they are intertwined all the way to the bottom, into a two-pronged plait (braid), showing the filling on top. Pinch the ends together to seal. Try not to pull at the lengths as you twist them, to prevent lengthening them too much.

Gently lift the babka into the lined loaf tin and cover with a clean dish towel. Leave to prove for 1 hour.

Preheat the oven to 200°C (180°C fan)/400°F/gas 6. Brush the loaves with olive oil, scatter with a little salt and bake for 35–40 minutes until golden and the base sounds hollow when tapped. Cool on a wire rack, then wrap in baking paper, secured with string.

Serves 6–8
–
Prep 25 mins
–
Cook 35–40 mins + resting, rising and proving

PRAWN BAGUETTES WITH PICKLED CUCUMBER & SRIRACHA P

A fresh light sandwich that packs a punch! The prawns can be replaced with finely sliced steak, white crabmeat, or silky braised aubergine.

2 tbsp rice vinegar
1 tsp caster (superfine) sugar
½ cucumber, shaved into ribbons
    with a peeler
10 radishes, thinly sliced
1 heaped tsp pickled ginger, shredded,
    plus extra to serve (optional)
4 small baguettes
mayonnaise, for spreading
1 baby gem lettuce, leaves shredded
150g (5½oz) small, cooked, peeled
    Atlantic (cold water) prawns (shrimp)
crispy onions, toasted sesame seeds
    and sriracha chilli sauce, to serve

Combine the rice vinegar and sugar in a large bowl. Toss in the cucumber ribbons, sliced radishes and ginger (if using) and set aside for at least 15 minutes before assembling your sandwiches (this quick pickle will keep well in the fridge for 1 day).

Assemble the sandwiches just before you head out to your picnic. Cut the baguettes open and spread with a little mayonnaise. Fill with shredded lettuce, the vegetables you pickled, then the prawns (shrimp). Wrap tightly in baking paper or foil, using string or rubber bands to secure, if needed. Also remember to pack a tub of store-bought crispy onions, some toasted sesame seeds, extra pickled ginger (if using) and a bottle of sriracha sauce for people to add before tucking in.

Serves 4
—
Prep 15 mins
+ pickling
time

GRILLED AUBERGINE SANDWICHES WITH CAPER, OLIVE & HERB SALSA VE

Silky soft marinated aubergines (eggplant) are one of my favourite things – that and salsa verde, which this salsa is a variation of. I could eat this combination every day and never tire of it.

1 large aubergine (eggplant),
   thinly sliced lengthways
extra virgin olive oil, for brushing
   and drizzling
1 red chilli, sliced
1 large garlic clove, sliced
4 pieces plain focaccia
   (store-bought, or see page 84)
sea salt and freshly ground
   black pepper

For the salsa
50g (1¾oz) pitted green olives,
   roughly chopped
1 tbsp capers, drained
handful of mint leaves
handful of parsley leaves
zest of ½ unwaxed lemon,
   peeled into thick strips
3 tbsp extra virgin olive oil

Brush the aubergine (eggplant) slices lightly with olive oil and cook on a griddle pan (ridged grill pan) over a high heat until charred and tender. Toss into a bowl with the chilli and garlic. Season with sea salt and drizzle generously with olive oil. Set aside. This can be done a day ahead, if you like – the aubergines will become even tastier if you do.

For the salsa, combine the olives, capers and herbs in a bowl. Cut the lemon zest into strips and add them to the bowl with the extra virgin olive oil. Season with salt.

To assemble the sandwiches, cut the focaccia pieces open and fill them with salsa and aubergine slices. Wrap tightly in greaseproof paper or foil to take on your picnic – you want the tasty oil to soak into the bread.

Serves 4
–
Prep 10 mins
–
Cook 15 mins

SMOKED HAM SANDWICHES WITH KIMCHI SLAW

Comfort food at its best. I recommend bringing some bottles of chilled lager and a packet of salt and vinegar crisps to go with these.

1 carrot, cut into thin matchsticks
5cm (2in) daikon (white radish),
    cut into thin matchsticks
10 mint leaves, larger leaves torn
2 spring onions (scallions), shredded
100g (3½oz) kimchi, shredded
8 slices seeded sourdough, or any
    other sliced bread you like
softened butter, for spreading
8 slices thick-cut smoked ham
sea salt

First make the slaw by combining the carrot, daikon, mint, spring onion (scallion) and kimchi in a bowl. Taste, adding a little salt if needed. Cover and chill until needed.

Just before leaving for your picnic, spread the bread with butter and simply make sandwiches filled with ham and slaw. Cut the sandwiches in half and sit them upright in a baking paper-lined container or two; if you pack them in tightly they will retain their shape when you come to unpack them at the picnic.

Serves 4
–
Prep 15
mins

PORCHETTA SANDWICHES WITH FENNEL & APPLE SALAD

Roasting a whole piece of pork belly to make a sandwich might sound excessive but think of this as the centrepiece of your picnic. I like to serve it with the Crushed Roasted Potato Salad on page 54, followed by the Peaches in Wine with Thyme Ricciarelli on page 128, for a pretty epic picnic. Cooking the pork rind (skin) separately makes the porchetta much easier to carve and helps achieve extra-crispy crackling.

20g (¾oz) bunch sage, leaves picked and finely chopped
4 sprigs rosemary, leaves picked and finely chopped
1 tsp fennel seeds
2 garlic cloves, finely chopped
2 tbsp olive oil
1.2kg (2lb 10oz) piece boned pork belly (you'll need the rind/skin, but ask your butcher to separate it from the meat and score it for you)
sea salt and freshly ground black pepper
8 ciabatta rolls and garlic mayonnaise, to serve

For the fennel and apple salad
1 fennel bulb, thinly sliced
1 Granny Smith apple, thinly sliced
juice of 1 lemon
olive oil, to drizzle

Preheat the oven to 200°C (180°C fan)/400°F/gas 6. Put the sage, rosemary and fennel seeds in a bowl with the garlic and 1 tbsp of the oil. Lay the pork onto a chopping board, rind-side-down, then rub the herb mixture all over the flesh. Season with salt and freshly ground black pepper.

Roll the meat into a long sausage shape and tie securely several times with kitchen string. Rub the outside with salt and pepper. Rub the remaining 1 tbsp of oil over the scored rind and season.

Lay the meat into a large roasting tin (pan) with the rind draped over it (this will help keep the meat moist), cook for 20 minutes, then reduce the oven temperature to 180°C (160°C fan)/350°F/gas 4 and cook for a further 2½ hours. When there are 30 minutes of cooking time remaining, move the crackling to one side and baste the porchetta with the cooking juices in the tin, to give it a chance to brown.

Transfer the porchetta and crackling to a tray lined with kitchen paper. Once cooled all the way through, wrap in foil. The porchetta will keep for 3 hours at room temperature, or transfer to the fridge and keep for up to 3 days.

The fennel and apple salad benefits from being made just before you head out to your picnic. Simply put all of the ingredients in a bowl and toss in some salt and pepper to taste.

To assemble, spread the ciabatta rolls with garlic mayo, then fill with thinly sliced porchetta (be generous!) and the crispy apple and fennel salad. Wrap the sandwiches tightly in baking paper or foil, using string or rubber bands to secure. Break the crackling up into small pieces and pack them separately to serve on the side.

Serves 8
–
Prep 20 mins
–
Cook 2 hours 50 mins

HARISSA CHICKEN SANDWICH WITH ROASTED PEACHES

This sandwich is a joyful flavour explosion. As a bonus, you'll probably have more roasted peaches than you need – perfect for eating on another day with cheese or with a pork chop.

4 chicken thighs on the bone,
    skin on or off, as you prefer
1 tbsp harissa
2 tbsp honey
Juice of ½ lemon
3 ripe peaches or nectarines,
    cut into thick wedges
1 large red onion, thinly sliced
1 red chilli, sliced into rounds
½ tsp cumin seeds
½ tsp coriander seeds, lightly crushed
1 cinnamon stick, halved
2 tbsp soft brown sugar
2 tbsp sherry vinegar
1 large ciabatta loaf
mayonnaise, to taste
handful of rocket (arugula) leaves
sea salt and freshly ground
    black pepper

Preheat the oven to 200°C (180°C fan)/400°F/gas 6. Put the chicken thighs in a roasting tin (pan). Combine the harissa, honey and lemon juice and rub the mixture all over the thighs using your hands. Season with salt and set aside.

Put the peaches in a separate roasting tin in which they fit snugly in a single layer. Top with the onion, chilli, spices, sugar and vinegar. Season with salt and pepper and toss everything well to combine. Cover with foil.

Place the roasting tin with the chicken in the top half of the oven and the peaches on the shelf underneath. Cook for 35–40 minutes or until the chicken is cooked through (the juices will run clear when tested in the thickest part with a skewer). Uncover the peaches halfway through cooking to give them a chance to caramelize. Set aside to cool.

To assemble, shred the chicken and discard the bones. Cut the ciabatta loaf open and spread the base with mayonnaise. Top with a layer of roasted peaches, the chicken and some rocket (arugula), then spoon on any chicken cooking juices from the tin. Close the sandwich and wrap tightly in baking paper or foil, using string or rubber bands to secure. Take to the picnic with a serrated bread knife to slice your ciabatta into sandwiches.

Serves 6
–
Prep 10 mins
–
Cook 50 mins
+ cooling

REBEL CUCUMBER SANDWICHES P

Made with more butter and salty anchovies than is sensible, and cool cucumber for freshness and crunch, this recipe marries the unassuming cucumber sandwich with the wonderful Roman tradition of serving anchovies on bread with a big slab of butter. It's a rule breaker, and I highly recommend accompanying it with a chilled larger.

8 slices white or brown (whole wheat) bread
salted butter, softened, for spreading
1 cucumber, thinly sliced
8–12 anchovy fillets in olive oil
(depending on how salty you like it)

Cut the crusts off the bread slices and liberally butter them all. Arrange a layer of cucumber over 4 of the buttered slices of bread, then drape 2–3 anchovy fillets over the cucumber slices.

Top with the remaining bread slices, buttered-side-down, then cut each sandwich in half lengthways. Pack the prepared sandwiches in a container in which they fit snuggly and keep chilled until you head out.

Serves 4
–
Prep 10 mins
–
No cooking

SWEET THINGS

The recipes in this chapter are a celebration of spring and summer fruits. Being able to sit outdoors on a sunny day, watching the world go by while snacking on cherries or biting into a ripe apricot is a pleasure I never take for granted. Pair them with a glass of chilled rosé and you have the most joyful of picnics.

GOOSEBERRY & ELDERFLOWER TRAYBAKE v

Gooseberries have such a short season that every bite of this traybake feels like a real treat, and a taste of British summer. Substitute raspberries or cherries when gooseberries are not in season.

125g (4½oz) self-raising flour
75g (2½oz) ground almonds
   (almond meal)
100g (3½oz) soft light brown sugar
150g (5½oz) butter, melted,
   plus extra for greasing
2 eggs, lightly beaten
75g (2½oz) natural yoghurt
grated zest of ½ unwaxed lemon
3 tbsp elderflower cordial,
   plus extra for the icing (frosting)
150g (5½oz) gooseberries
2 tbsp granulated sugar
15g (½oz) flaked almonds
2 tbsp icing (confectioners') sugar
crème fraîche (or mascarpone spiked
   with a few tablespoons of sweet
   muscat wine), to serve

Preheat the oven to 180°C (160°C fan)/350°F/gas 4. Grease and line a 20cm x 15cm (8in x 6in) cake tin (pan).

In a large mixing bowl, use a wooden spoon to combine the flour, ground almonds (almond meal), brown sugar, butter, eggs, yoghurt, lemon zest and elderflower cordial. Beat until smooth. Scrape the batter into the prepared cake tin and level the surface using a palette knife.

Toss the gooseberries in half of the granulated sugar, then gently arrange them on top of the batter, spaced evenly. Scatter the remaining granulated sugar and the flaked almonds over the top and bake for 40–45 minutes, or until a skewer inserted into the centre comes out clean. Allow to cool in the tin.

To make the icing (frosting), put the icing (confectioners') sugar in a small bowl and mix in just enough elderflower cordial to form a thin paste with a drizzling consistency. Drizzle liberally over the cake.

It's easiest to take the cake to the picnic in its tin, but you can cut it into 12 pieces beforehand, and wrap to take with you. Serve with crème fraîche or, if you're feeling indulgent, mascarpone spiked with sweet muscat wine.

WIMBLEDON BUNS V

Wimbledon week in London is all about watching the tennis while enjoying the long hours of daylight, sipping Pimm's and eating the sweetest English strawberries drowned in cream. These cheeky buns are inspired by the mood of those lazy days and, served with my Rebel Cucumber Sandwiches (see page 104), they make the most quaint, if inauthentic, afternoon picnic tea.

400g (14oz) strawberries
3 tbsp caster (superfine) sugar
2 tbsp Pimm's
300ml (1¼ cups) whipping cream
6 brioche rolls

Remove and discard the green leafy tops of the strawberries, slice and put the strawberries in the container they will travel in. Stir in 1 tbsp of the sugar and the Pimm's. Cover and keep chilled.

Pour the cream into a large bowl. Sift in the remaining 2 tbsp sugar and whisk until the cream just holds its shape when the whisk is removed. Spoon into the container it will travel in, cover and keep chilled.

Once at the picnic, split the brioche buns open. Spoon a little of the strawberry juices into the buns, then add a layer of sliced strawberries and a generous dollop of cream. You could also assemble the buns at home and arrange them in a baking tray (sheet pan), see opposite, if you don't have far to travel.

Makes 6
—
Prep
15 mins

PLUM & RICOTTA PASTRIES v

Making these is child's play, but they really are delicious, and light and delicate too, thanks to the zesty ricotta that sits beneath the plums.

125g (4½oz) ricotta
grated zest of ½ unwaxed lemon
2 tbsp icing (confectioners') sugar
1 × 320g (11¼oz) sheet ready-rolled
    puff pastry, defrosted if frozen
plain (all-purpose) flour, for dusting
6 ripe plums, halved and pitted
1 tbsp milk, for glazing
2 tbsp maple syrup
25g (1oz) flaked almonds

Preheat the oven to 200°C (180°C fan)/400°F/gas 6 with a shelf positioned in the centre of the oven.

Put the ricotta and lemon zest in a bowl. Sift in the icing (confectioners') sugar and stir well to combine.

Unroll the pastry onto a worktop lightly dusted with flour. Use a cookie cutter or upturned glass to cut out twelve 8cm (3¼in) pastry rounds. Transfer the rounds to a baking tray (sheet pan) lined with baking paper and place 1 tsp of ricotta mixture on the centre of each round. Sit a plum half on top of each, cut-side-down. Brush the pastry border with milk and bake in the preheated oven, on the heated shelf, for 20 minutes.

Pull the baking tray out of the oven and gently remove the loosened skins from the plums and discard them. Brush the fruit and pastry with the maple syrup, then scatter with the flaked almonds and return to the oven for a further 5–8 minutes, or until golden. Cool on a wire rack.

These can be baked up to 1 day ahead of the picnic and stored in an airtight container once cooled. They are quite delicate, so use a large shallow container and place a sheet of baking paper between layers if you are stacking them.

Makes 12
–
Prep 15 mins
–
Cook 25 mins

BLUEBERRY & RASPBERRY LOAF CAKE v

No cake is easier to pack for a picnic than a loaf cake. This one has a light moist crumb and a lovely crunchy top. I serve it on its own, with a thick Greek or coconut yoghurt.

175g (6oz) unsalted butter, softened, plus extra for greasing
250g (9oz) self-raising flour
150g (5½oz) caster (superfine) sugar
3 eggs, lightly beaten
1 tsp vanilla extract
150g (5½oz) blueberries
150g (5½oz) raspberries
25g (1oz) flaked almonds
2 tbsp demerara sugar

Preheat the oven to 170°C (150°C fan)/325°F/gas 3. Grease and line a 900g (2lb) cake tin (pan) with baking paper.

Put the flour in a large bowl, then add the butter, sugar, eggs and vanilla extract. Beat together with an electric mixer for 4–5 minutes until pale and fluffy.

Gently fold through the berries and spoon the batter into the tin. Scatter the flaked almonds and demerara sugar over the top, then bake for 1 hour 15 minutes to 1 hour 30 minutes, or until a skewer inserted into the centre comes out clean. Cool in the tin for 15 minutes, then turn out onto a wire rack and cool completely.

Pack the cake back into the tin to make sure it travels to your picnic in one piece. The cake will keep well for 2 days.

Serves 10–12
–
Prep 15 mins
–
Cook 1hr 15 –
1 hr 30 mins

Sweet Things

FIG & CHERRY CARDAMOM FRIANDS v

I much prefer friands to cupcakes and muffins. They're pretty impossible to mess up, plus when I'm in the mood for something sweet, just one little friand is enough to hit the spot. Feel free to swap the fruit for anything you have at home: nectarines, raspberries, apricots, even a slice of lemon.

110g (3¾oz) unsalted butter, melted, plus extra for greasing
90g (3¼oz) plain (all-purpose) flour, plus extra for dusting
5 cardamom pods
125g (4½oz) pistachios (shelled weight)
½ tsp baking powder
190g (6¾oz) icing (confectioners') sugar, sifted
5 egg whites
3 tbsp caster (superfine) sugar
3 figs, cut into wedges
handful of cherries, pitted

Preheat the oven to 160°C (140°fan)/320°F/gas 3. Butter and flour a non-stick 12-hole muffin tin (pan).

Bash the cardamom pods open with the side of a cook's knife and prise out the seeds (discard the pods). Blitz the cardamom seeds and pistachios in the bowl of a food processor until the pistachios are finely ground. Add the remaining ingredients except for the fruit and blitz for about 1 minute, until nice and foamy.

Spoon the mixture into the prepared muffin tin, then arrange the fruit and pistachios on top. I like to switch it up, so some will have a cherry or two, others a wedge of fig, but most get cherry and fig. Bake for 20–25 minutes until light golden and springy to the touch.

Remove from the oven and leave in the tin for 5 minutes before turning out onto a wire rack to cool. Once cooled, they are ready to pack.

Makes 12
–
Prep 30 mins
–
Cook 20–25 mins

PASSION FRUIT & COCONUT SLICES v

A winning combination: a crumbly shortbread biscuit base topped with passion fruit and coconut, flavours that remind me so much of Brazilian desserts. These don't last long around my kids.

For the biscuit base

165g (5¾oz) lightly salted butter, softened
4 tbsp caster (superfine) sugar
200g (7oz) plain (all-purpose) flour

For the passion fruit and coconut layer

100ml (3½fl oz) passion fruit pulp, seeds included (about 4 passion fruit)
2 tbsp lime juice
4 eggs
300g (10½oz) caster (superfine) sugar
80g (2¾oz) desiccated (shredded) coconut
2 tbsp plain (all-purpose) flour

Preheat the oven to 180°C (160°C fan)/350°F/gas 4. Line a 20cm x 25cm (8in x 10in) baking tray (sheet pan) with baking paper, letting the paper come up the sides.

In a large bowl, beat together the butter and sugar for the base using an electric whisk or a wooden spoon until well combined. Sift in the flour and slowly mix to form a soft dough. Transfer the dough to the prepared tray and, using the palm of your hand, press it down firmly to cover the base in an even, compact layer. Bake for 30 minutes or until the top is lightly golden, then set aside to cool. Leave the oven on.

To make the passion fruit and coconut layer, use a fork to whisk together the passion fruit, lime juice and eggs, then stir in the sugar, coconut and flour and mix until well combined. Carefully pour the topping mixture over the cooled biscuit base, return to the oven and bake for a further 35–40 minutes, until set and lightly golden. Leave to cool completely before cutting into 16 slices.

Makes 16
—
Prep 15 mins
—
Cook 1 hour 10 mins + cooling

JAM LATTICE TART v

Tarts like this were a staple when I was growing up in Italy, either homemade or bought from the local *pasticceria*. Call it nostalgia, but sitting on a blanket eating a slice of jam (fruit preserve) tart, while trying to avoid getting any on my t-shirt makes me feel 5 years old again.

300g (10½oz) plain (all-purpose) flour, plus extra for dusting
85g (3oz) icing (confectioners') sugar, plus extra for dusting
pinch of salt
150g (5½oz) unsalted butter, cubed and chilled
grated zest of ½ unwaxed orange
2 eggs, lightly beaten, plus 1 egg, beaten, for glazing
500g (1lb 2oz) of your jam (fruit preserve) of choice (I've used wild strawberry jam)

For the pastry, put the flour, sugar and salt into the bowl of a food processor. Pulse until the dry ingredients are well combined. Add the butter and orange zest and pulse again, until the butter is incorporated and the mixture resembles coarse breadcrumbs. Finally, add the 2 lightly beaten eggs and pulse until the dough comes together. If it's still too crumbly, add 1 tbsp cold water, in stages, until the dough just comes together. Tip the dough out of the mixer and shape into two discs, one slightly larger than the other. Wrap in cling film (plastic wrap) and chill for 1 hour until firm.

Preheat the oven to 200°C (180°C fan)/400°F/gas 6 and place a baking sheet in the oven to heat up. On a lightly floured worktop, roll out the larger pastry disc to 0.5cm (¼in) thick and use to line a 23cm (9in) fluted tart tin (pan). Trim the edges and bring together all the trimmings, wrap again and chill. Place the lined tart tin in the fridge to chill.

Now roll out the remaining pastry disc in the same way, this time on a sheet of baking paper. Using a sharp knife or pizza cutter, cut out 2cm (¾in) wide strips. Repeat with the chilled pastry trimmings, to give you more strips. You'll need about 14 in total. Slide a baking sheet under the baking paper to help carry the strips to the fridge, to chill for 15 minutes.

Remove the chilled pastry case and strips from the fridge. Spoon the jam (fruit preserve) into the pastry case, evening it out with the back of a spoon. Now add your lattice. Weave the strips of pastry evenly over the jam to create a lattice pattern and push them into the edge of the tart. Trim away the overhanging pastry. Use the remaining lightly beaten egg to brush the top of the lattice.

Transfer the tart to the oven, sitting it on the heated baking sheet. Bake for 10 minutes, then reduce the oven temperature to 170°C (150°C fan)/325°F/gas 3 and bake for a further 30–35 minutes until the pastry is golden and the filling is bubbling.

Remove the tart from the oven and sit it on a wire rack to cool completely. To take the tart to the picnic, dust it with icing (confectioners') sugar, then wrap it loosely in baking paper and carry it on a tray, board or large platter.

Serves 10
–
Prep 30 mins
+ chilling
–
Cook 40–45 mins

APRICOT FRANGIPANE GALETTE V

Simple and classic, this galette can also be made with nectarines, plums, or even canned pears.

75g (2½oz) unsalted butter, softened
50g (1¾oz) caster (superfine) sugar
2 eggs, 1 whole, 1 lightly beaten
    for glazing
100g (3½oz) ground almonds
    (almond meal)
1 × 320g (11¼oz) sheet ready-rolled
    puff pastry, defrosted if frozen
5–6 ripe apricots, stoned and
    thinly sliced
2 tbsp demerara sugar

For the frangipane, use an electric mixer to cream together the butter and sugar in a mixing bowl. Crack in the whole egg and mix to combine. Add the ground almonds (almond meal) and mix to make a smooth paste. Cover and chill until needed.

Unroll the pastry onto a baking tray (sheet pan) lined with baking paper. Evenly spread the frangipane onto the pastry, leaving a 5cm (2in) border. Arrange the sliced apricots over the frangipane – you can fan them out, or simply scatter them over the top haphazardly. Fold the pastry border up and over the fruit to partially enclose and chill for 30 minutes.

Preheat the oven to 220°C (200°C fan)/425°F/gas 7. Brush the edges of the pastry with the beaten egg, then scatter over the demerara sugar. Bake for 10 minutes, reduce the temperature to 200°C (180°C fan)/400°F/gas 6, and cook for a further 20 minutes, until the pastry is cooked through, crisp and golden (cover the top with a piece of foil if it starts to colour too quickly).

Leave to cool on a wire rack then wrap in baking paper and foil for your picnic. Eat on the day of baking.

Serves 4–6
–
Prep 20 mins
–
Cook 30 mins
+ cooling

Sweet Things

GRAPE, LEMON & THYME FOCACCIA VE

A lovely, sweet-savoury focaccia that I like to serve, instead of dessert, with an oozy cheese such as a brie or camembert.

Focaccia dough (see page 84)

For the topping
2 tbsp olive oil
zest of 1 unwaxed lemon,
    peeled into thick strips
handful of thyme leaves
400g (14oz) black grapes
1 tbsp granulated sugar

The day before you plan to bake your focaccia, follow the method for the Plain Focaccia recipe (see page 84), up to the point where the dough has proved and you have added dimples to the surface with your fingertips and poured the brine over it.

Preheat the oven to 200°C (180°C fan)/400°F/gas 6, with a shelf positioned in the centre of the oven.

For the topping, pour the olive oil into a small bowl and stir in the lemon zest and thyme. Set aside.

Scatter the grapes over the focaccia and gently push them into the dough. Sprinkle the sugar over the top.

Bake the focaccia in the preheated oven, on the heated shelf, for 25 minutes. Spoon over the lemon and thyme oil and return to the oven, turning the tray around so that the focaccia bakes evenly. Bake for a further 10–15 minutes until golden. Cool on a wire rack.

The focaccia is best eaten on the day of baking, but will keep in an airtight container for up to 2 days.

Serves 10–12
–
Prep 15 mins
+ overnight
chilling, resting
and proving
–
Cook 40 mins

SEASONAL FRUITS WITH RICOTTA, HONEY & GRANOLA v

This lovely platter makes a delicious casual dessert but would work just as well as a stand-alone dish for a mid-morning or late-afternoon picnic. Help yourself to a scoop of honey-drizzled ricotta and your fruit of choice, and scatter with a little granola.

250g (9oz) tub ricotta
selection of fresh ripe fruit
honey, to drizzle
granola, to serve

Take all the elements to your picnic in separate containers – or if you're staying close to home, prepare your platter just before leaving and carry it carefully to your chosen spot.

Pour out any liquid from the ricotta tub, then turn the ricotta out onto a large platter. Arrange a selection of fruits around it. Think of flavours and colours that go well together, such as apricots, raspberries and cherries, or plums and blackberries. You'll also need a jar of honey and a small bowl of granola for sprinkling.

Drizzle honey over the ricotta, sprinkle over the granola and enjoy.

Serves 4–6
–
Prep
5 mins

Sweet Things

PEACHES IN WINE WITH THYME RICCIARELLI v

Peaches in wine is a classic Italian summer dessert. Traditionally the sugared fruit and wine are macerated together in advance, but I like keeping them separate until the last minute, for a fresher flavour. I serve them with ricciarelli, Sienese almond biscuits that I've livened up with thyme, which goes really well with summer stone fruit.

For the ricciarelli
300g (10½oz) blanched almonds
325g (11½oz) icing (confectioners') sugar
2 tsp thyme leaves
finely grated zest of ½ unwaxed lemon
85g (3oz) caster (superfine) sugar
2 medium egg whites

For the peaches in wine
4 ripe peaches
1 tbsp caster (superfine) sugar
1 bottle chilled dry white wine, such as pinot grigio or sauvignon blanc

Make the dough for the ricciarelli 1 day ahead. Tip the almonds into the bowl of a food processor. Add 225g (8oz) of the icing (confectioners') sugar and blitz until the almonds are ground, but still have a little more texture than store-bought ground almonds (almond meal). Transfer to a large bowl and stir in the thyme, lemon zest and caster (superfine) sugar. Set aside.

In a separate bowl, whisk the egg whites using an electric whisk until they form stiff peaks.

Stir the egg whites into the almond mixture, cover the bowl with cling film (plastic wrap) and chill overnight. The mixture needs to be well chilled so that it keeps its shape in the oven and cooks to the right texture.

The next day, preheat the oven to 200°C (180°C fan)/400°F/ gas 6 and line two baking trays (sheet pans) with baking paper. Dust the remaining 100g (3½oz) icing sugar onto a large plate. Take a heaped tbsp of dough (about 30g/1oz) and roll it into a sausage shape between your hands. Roll the dough in the icing sugar, making sure it's coated in a thick layer.

Put it on one of the lined baking trays and flatten it very slightly with the palm of your hand, so that it's about 1.5cm (⅝in) thick. Repeat with the remaining dough, making sure to leave some room between each biscuit to spread as they bake. You should have enough dough to make about 20 ricciarelli. Bake for 10–12 minutes, or until lightly golden with a crackled appearance. They'll still be soft, but will set once cooled.

Leave to cool on the trays for 5 minutes, then transfer to a wire rack to cool completely. Store in a portable airtight container.

Cut the peaches into wedges and put them into a portable container with a waterproof lid. Gently stir in the sugar, cover and keep chilled until you leave for your picnic.

To serve, turn the peach wedges in their macerating juices, then divide them between 6 glasses, adding any juices left behind. Pour some wine over the fruit, so that it's partly submerged, and serve with the ricciarelli.

Serves 6
–
Prep 15 mins
–
Cook 10–12 mins + overnight chilling

DRINKS

It's easy to grab a beer or a bottle of wine on your way to a picnic, but nothing announces a good time more than pulling out a jug or bottle of a sunny homemade drink. Unless, that is, you pull a whole load of lovely ripe fruit, a bottle of rosé and some ice out of your cool-bag instead and make sangria on site.

PASSION FRUIT, COCONUT & LIME BATIDA (OR 'NOT FOR KIDS') VE

I first created this drink, adapted from the Brazilian *cachaça* cocktail, traditionally made with either passion fruit, limes or coconut, to take to a party. I combined the three classic batida flavours into one, poured it into a bottle and was almost out of the door when it dawned on me that it looked dangerously like orange squash. My husband, Nick, quickly scribbled 'Not for kids' on the bottle, and a brand was born.

8 passion fruit
4 unwaxed limes
450ml (2 cups) coconut water
200ml (scant 1 cup) cachaça or vodka
3 tbsp caster (superfine) sugar

I make this in a large screw-top jar or bottle with a wide enough opening for the ingredients to go in easily.

Cut the passion fruit in half and scoop the pulp into the jar or bottle. Quarter the limes, squeeze in the juice, dropping the squeezed quarters in as well. Add the remaining ingredients, screw on the lid and give the bottle a good, vigorous shake. You could strain the mixture now, but I like to let it sit for at least 30 minutes in the fridge for the lime wedges to continue adding flavour to the drink.

Strain into individual sealable bottles and chill. Ideally you want to drink it ice-cold, so I tend to pop the bottles into the freezer, avoiding the risk of it warming up too much in transit. It has a high alcohol content so although it might turn to slush, it shouldn't fully freeze.

Serves 6
–
Prep 10 mins

ORANGE EARL GREY ICED TEA v

This tea has a lovely floral flavour. Cold brewing iced tea is a tip I learned from Catherine Phipps, in her book *Leaf*. The result is mellow, without even a hint of bitterness and totally worth the forward planning.

2 tbsp orange blossom honey
5 earl grey tea bags
zest of 1 unwaxed orange, peeled into thick strips, plus 1 sliced unwaxed orange, to serve
1 tsp orange blossom water (optional)
ice (optional)

The evening before your picnic, put the honey in a large jug (pitcher). Stir in 1–2 tbsp boiling water from the kettle (use just enough to dissolve the honey) then pour in 1 litre (4⅓ cups) cold water and drop in the tea bags and pared orange zest. Chill in the fridge overnight.

The next day, fish out the tea bags and orange zest (discard) and stir in the orange blossom water, if using. Taste, adding more honey or orange blossom water if needed. Transfer the tea to a large sealable bottle (or individual bottles or jam jars). Keep chilled until you leave on your picnic.

Serve with orange slices and ice if it's lost its chill.

Makes 1 litre
(4⅓ cups)
–
Prep 5 mins
+ overnight
brewing

Drinks

MINT LEMON- LIMEADE VE

The whizzed-up zest and sugar in this lemonade takes citrus-zingy-pop to another level. If you have a lemon tree or can find a lemon with a leaf attached, add the leaf when making the sugar for an added mellow floral note. For an alcoholic cocktail, just add a dash of vodka or rum.

4 unwaxed limes
4 unwaxed lemons
10 mint leaves
60g (2¼oz) granulated sugar
1 lemon leaf (if available)

To serve
sparkling water
unwaxed lemon and lime slices
mint leaves
ice

Peel large strips of zest from 1 lemon and 1 lime. Whizz the zests in a food processor with the mint leaves, sugar and, if you have one, the lemon leaf. Once well combined, spoon half the flavoured sugar into a large jug (pitcher).

Squeeze the juice of the remaining limes and lemons into the jug and stir well to encourage the sugar to dissolve. Pour in sparkling water to taste, adding more of the zesty flavoured sugar if you think it needs it (any leftover flavoured sugar will keep in the fridge for a couple of days). Chill.

If your picnic is so close to home that you can take it in the jug, brilliant – add some ice and slices of lemon and lime, and you're ready to go. Alternatively, pour the drink into a sealable bottle and take the sliced citrus and mint with you in a separate container. Add them to serving glasses with ice, then pour in the lemon-limeade.

Serves 6–8
–
Prep 10
mins

WATERMELON AGUA FRESCA VE

This thirst-quenching *agua fresca* is exactly the kind of drink you'll want on a summer's-day picnic.

1.2kg (2lb 12oz) watermelon
   (whole weight)
1 tbsp agave syrup, honey
   or caster (superfine) sugar
4 mint leaves
sea salt
juice of 2 limes

To serve
unwaxed lime wedges
mint leaves
sparkling water
ice

Remove the flesh from the watermelon and put it in a blender with the agave syrup and mint leaves. Add a pinch of salt and 350ml (1½ cups) water and blend. Strain through a fine sieve (strainer) lined with muslin (cheesecloth), discard the solids, then pour the liquid into a large sealable bottle and chill.

Take on your picnic and serve with lime wedges, mint leaves, sparkling water and ice, if you have some.

Serves 6–8
–
Prep 10
mins

ROSÉ
SANGRIA VE

Lighter and sunnier than sangria made with red wine, and all the more delicious for it.

2 peaches or nectarines,
   cut into wedges
200g (7oz) strawberries,
   hulled and sliced
1 unwaxed orange, cut into chunks
1 tbsp caster (superfine) sugar
1 bottle dry rosé wine
50ml (3½ tbsp) Cointreau or
   Grand Marnier (if you have it
   at home; leave it out otherwise)
12 mint leaves
200–300ml (scant 1 cup–1¼ cups)
   chilled sparkling water
ice cubes

There are two ways of making this drink: at home in a jug (pitcher), or at the picnic.

If making it at home, combine all the ingredients except the sparkling water and ice in a jug/pitcher (ideally one with a lid so it is easier to transport) and keep chilled for at least 1 hour to allow the flavours to develop before heading out. Stir in 300ml (1¼ cups) sparkling water and ice at the picnic, just before serving.

If you're making the sangria at the picnic, chill the fruit in advance and keep it cool. Cut it up at the picnic and stir all the ingredients except the sparkling water into a jug, along with 5 ice cubes. The challenge is then to wait until the ice cubes have melted a bit before pouring in 200ml (scant 1 cup) sparkling water, giving the sangria a bit of time to macerate and chill before drinking.

Serves 6
–
**Prep 10 mins
+ macerating
time**

INDEX

ACKNOWLEDGEMENTS

The irony of working on a picnic cookbook in winter, during lockdown, was not lost on me when writing this book. Picnics are all about coming together, so if I'm honest, at first, it felt a little lonely. But what a joy when lockdown was finally lifted, spring exploded into our lives and the loveliest of teams came together to photograph the book. Cookbook photoshoots are always fun, but this one was bursting with positive energy, laughter and good people. And they all loved the food! Hurray!

I'd like to thank the shoot team for bringing my ideas to life and making work such a pleasure. Louie Waller for your beautiful prop styling and flair. Jo Cowan for letting us raid your cupboards, wardrobe and kitchen cabinets for all things flowy and picnicy (and just being the loveliest hostess). Peaches, the cat, for making us laugh every time you photobombed the set with your fabulous yoga poses. Sonali Shah, you superstar! I couldn't have wished for a better righthand woman: not only cooking like a demon, but also tasting, tweaking and bringing your brilliant ideas to the table. Becky Wilkinson, I can't believe you made time in your crazy-busy life to come help out for a day. Looking forward to picnicking together on your narrowboat home soon! Laura Edwards, the dapple queen, who always goes above and beyond while making it all look so effortless (whether shooting in your calm studio or in the Hackney Marshes, being attacked by all the creatures). And, of course, Max and Nina, for stepping in to do a bit of modelling. Thank you all!

Thank you to the team at Quadrille. Sarah Lavelle for being so supportive as I embarked on this project. Stacey Cleworth for your infinite patience and being so flexible with schedules and my constant swapping and changing. Emily Lapworth for your lovely design and art direction. Susan Low for your eagle-eyed attention to detail.

Annie Rigg, thank you for your generosity in letting me adapt your pork pie recipe for this book. And Lola Milne and Sonali for all your brilliant recipe testing.

Finally, thanks to Nick, Nina and Max for your patience, support and unedited feedback as I developed these recipes. And for not complaining when our kitchen (and house…) is taken over by my mess!